study daily

THE BOOK OF MORMON

ZACHARY COWAN

ISBN: 1546391800
ISBN-13: 978-1546391807

ACKNOWLEDGMENTS

I willingly acknowledge that any good idea or question in this book is the result of inspiration from Heavenly Father and Jesus Christ through the ministration of the Holy Ghost. However, any and all bad ones are the result of my own stupidity. I would like to thank my Girlface for never thinking more or less of me, but for always seeing me for who I really am. I love you. I express my love to my four rapscallion boys: Quinn, Maxwell, Oliver, and Sullivan. They are positive they are famous, for now their names are in a book. Thanks to Launa Albrecht for her cover design, and her appreciated advice. To my wonderful editors and friends Mary Einfeldt, and Brian Passey I offer my gratitude for their encouragement, and lack of eye-rolls each time they fixed one of my many errors.

Table of Contents

Introduction. 1

Books of the Book of Mormon

1 Nephi. 3

2 Nephi. 19

Jacob. 38

Enos. 43

Jarom. 44

Omni. 44

The Words of Mormon. 45

Mosiah. 46

Alma. 62

Helaman. 114

3 Nephi. 125

4 Nephi. 141

Mormon. 142

Ether. 148

Moroni. 159

Bibliography. 165

Introduction

After desiring to see the things which his father saw, Nephi found himself on top of an unfamiliar mountain. If ever there were a need for an experienced mountain guide it would be now. The Spirit of the God, in the form of a man, and an unnamed angel would appear shortly and serve as personal Sherpas to Nephi on this journey. As good guides do, these two would frequently direct Nephi's attention to important details by asking him questions, and asking him to "look" for specific things. The purpose of this book is to serve as a guide as you study the Book of Mormon. It will provide direction to your studying, that you might find the insight and direction that God has to help you ascend and descend the unfamiliar mountains of your life.

How can this book be helpful to the youth, and seminary students?

Youth are often taught to study the scriptures, but many have never been taught how to study, so they spend their time reading the scriptures. When they do this they occasionally find a gem, but the context and even the content of this jewel is often misunderstood. Thus, most youth have a spiritual experience reading scriptures, but they do not receive all of the rich and powerful blessings associated with studying the scriptures.

In your Topical Guide look up "Scriptures, Study of." Don't worry about looking up any of these verses, just read through what is there and use the space below to make a list of words that describe how the scriptures should be studied.

_____

_____

_____

_____

_____

_____

_____

The very next entry in the Topical Guide is "Scriptures, Value of." As you read through these make a list of all the Lord's promises for studying the scriptures and not just reading them.

_____

_____

_____

_____

_____

_____

_____

How can this book help adults?

While adults often understand the context and content of the scriptures better than most youth, many of them still struggle to see how to apply the scriptures. This is a skill that can be developed, just like any other. The questions in this book will help all individuals, regardless of age or gospel maturity, to better understand and apply the scriptures.

How can this book help families?

This book makes family scripture study more convenient. The daily portions are manageable and the questions allow for both discovery and discussion. This book provides a great way to follow along with your seminary students in their studies or to start discussions at the dinner table. Many youth might feel more inclined to answer a question if they feel that it is not coming from their parents. This book could be given to the children, and they could be asked to prepare questions to present to their parents or to direct a family discussion. Couples may also find strength and enjoyment through reading and discussing these sections together.

How can this book help teachers?

If you have ever run out of gas, you know how impossible it is to drive. Many teachers struggle in the classroom to have meaningful discussion and impact because they do not know the type of questions that fill the tank. Many of the questions in this book allow students to first search the scriptures and then, with a full tank, teachers and students can engage in more meaningful discussions about the words and ideas of the scriptures. As their understanding becomes clearer, it will be easier to see how the principles can apply to their own lives. This pattern is demonstrated in most of the daily entries.

Day 1, 1 Nephi 1:1-15

I am very excited to study the Book of Mormon with you, so let's get to it. No other family gets more pages devoted to the telling of their story than the family of Lehi and Sariah. We will see this family and its members face all kinds of situations that we can learn from, both good and bad. Today's section is no exception. What can you learn about family life from the famous verse 1?

What similarities do you see between Lehi's experience and that of Joseph Smith's? Are there other prophets who have had similar experiences?

A phrase that has caused many people to wonder is: "and he thought he saw God sitting upon his throne" (:8). Did he, or did he not see God? This phrase is actually an ancient form of writing and expression used by people who were so careful about keeping the commandment "not to take the name of the Lord thy God in vain" that they wouldn't even write it the name Jehovah, but instead used the words Lord and God (Exodus 20:7).

In verse 12, notice what results come from reading sacred books from heaven. Have you ever experienced this same thing? If you are prayerful and careful I hope that this will be your experience every day in the Book of Mormon.

Day 2, 1 Nephi 1:16-2:15

In 1 Nephi 1:16-20 we are given a great summary of Lehi's reaction to his vision and teaching. What things do you find impressive?

Elder David A. Bednar said, "I testify that the tender mercies of the Lord are real and that they do not occur randomly or merely by coincidence.

Often the Lord's timing of His tender mercies helps us to both discern and acknowledge them. ... The Lord's tender mercies are the very personal and individualized blessings, strength, protection, assurances, guidance, loving-kindness, consolation, support, and spiritual gifts which we receive from and because of and through the Lord Jesus Christ" (*Ensign*, May 2005, 99-100). Nephi wrote to show us these mercies, and Moroni concluded the Book of Mormon by asking us to think how merciful God has been (Moroni 10:3). To help us see how merciful God is to others and ourselves is one of the major purposes of the Book of Mormon. Pray that you notice them, be thankful for them, and let the tender mercies of the Lord change your life.

What examples of tender mercies have you or those you love had in the last week?

In 1 Nephi 2:1-15, look for all of the different reasons Lehi had to be disobedient to the Lord's commandment to leave. How well did Lehi follow his own counsel given to Laman and Lemuel in 1 Nephi 2:8-10?

In 1 Nephi 2:6-7, we are given two phrases that are grammatically interesting constructs incorrect in English, but are marvelous evidences of ancient forms of writing: "river of water" in verse 6, and "altar of stones" in 7. Only in the Middle East and other deserts are dry rivers commonly found. That is why a river of water is pointed out. A stone altar might denote that the rocks were cut or shaped, but the phrase "altar of stones" is evidence that the direction in Exodus 20:25 was followed. These are two little evidences that the book is true. They are fun, but not as important as "tender mercies."

Day 3, 1 Nephi 2:16-3:8

Most scholars believe that the distance that Lehi and his family have covered at this point in their journey is between 150-180 miles. Pay careful attention to what made the difference between Nephi and Laman and Lemuel. Why did Nephi not end up with their same feelings?

In addition to learning about Lehi's family, what subtle things does today's section teach you about commandments? There are several, but what did you see?

4

Day 4, 1 Nephi 3:9-31

In today's section we will see Nephi and his brothers make their first and second attempts at getting the plates. As you read, consider how many different attempts you are willing to make with what the Lord has asked you to do.

Verses 12, 19-20 contain Nephi's explanation of why they needed the plates. What do you think Nephi might add to his list in the next few years? What reasons might you add to that list?

In verse 21, Nephi had to "persuade" Laman and Lemuel to continue to try to get the plates. Are there commandments that you have to be persuaded to keep or attempt to keep? Which commandments are you like Nephi, persuading others to keep? Which commandments do you, like Laman and Lemuel, need persuading to keep?

Day 5, 1 Nephi 4:1-18

Even after seeing an angel, Laman and Lemuel were still afraid of Laban and his power to control 50 men (3:31). In verses 1-3, look for what Nephi said about Laban's power. What local problems, people, and issues could you have more confidence in the Lord to help you with?

What can we learn about following the spirit from the story in verses 4-18? The more carefully you read it the more you will discover.

How is Nephi not a murderer?

Day 6, 1 Nephi 4:19-5:6

How is Nephi not a thief and a liar? This quote from Joseph Smith is very helpful: "That which is wrong under one circumstance, may be, and often is, right under another. God said, 'Thou shalt not kill'; at another time He said, 'Thou shalt utterly destroy.' This is the principle on which the government of heaven is conducted—by revelation adapted to the circumstances in which the children of the kingdom are placed. Whatever God requires is right, no matter what it is, although we may not see the reason thereof till long after the events transpire." (*Teachings of the Joseph Smith*, 256). This is a very dangerous quote, unless you know how to follow the Spirit. Nephi did. How well do you trust your own abilities to feel and recognize the Spirit?

As you read this familiar story of Nephi getting the plates, consider it this time as the conversion story of Zoram. Does that change the way you read it? What do you think he was feeling as Nephi was holding him and talking to him, even making an oath?

As the boys have been gone, things have not been well at camp. In 1 Nephi 5:1-6, look for things that helped a marriage—and a mother—during this time. How have those things been used, or how could those things be used by you in difficult circumstances or times of stress?

Day 7, 1 Nephi 5:7-6:6

Yesterday we saw how Lehi's testimony helped provide comfort and support to him and Sariah while the boys were gone. In 1 Nephi 5:7-9, look for evidence that Sariah's testimony has grown from this hard experience. Think of your hard experiences: What lessons did you learn from them?

Read 1 Nephi 5:10-6:3 and look for what Lehi found upon the brass plates. Notice that studying the scriptures was not simply an experience about other people in other lands, it was about feeling the Spirit and being motivated to keep the commandments (1 Nephi 5:17, 21). What do you do to make scripture study personal?

What does Lehi promise and prophesy about the Bible in 1 Nephi 5:18-19? What does Nephi say about the purpose for the Book of Mormon in 1 Nephi 6:3-6? What insights did you get by looking at the promises, prophecies, and purposes of those great books?

Day 8, 1 Nephi 7:1-15

Why do you think the Lord had them get the scriptures before wives? How could that help them in their marriages?

If they were 180 miles away before they went to get the plates, how many miles will they have traveled by the time they are done getting the brass plates and wives? Why do you think the Lord didn't have them pick up everything before they left the first time?

Notice what Nephi did to get Ishmael and this family to leave their old lives behind (7:3-5). What lessons can we learn from those verses about helping other progress on their journey?

How is rebellion different from making a mistake? What do we learn from verses 6-15 about the reasons for and causes of rebellion? What would happen to others if you forgot and rebelled against God?

Day 9, 1 Nephi 7:16-8:18

What can 1 Nephi 7:16-19 teach us about being helped and delivered by the Atonement? Look for what Nephi asked for versus what he received.

In family life there is almost a continual need for forgiveness. How can Nephi's example in 1 Nephi 7:20-22 help us to forgive more?

Chapter 8 shows us how intertwined the gospel and family really are. From 1 Nephi 8:1-18, what insights do you learn about the link between gospel and family?

Do Lehi's descriptive words about the fruit in 1 Nephi 8:10-12 match your own experience with the gospel?

Day 10, 1 Nephi 8:19-38

As you read today's section, look for the things that led people to the tree, and for things that led them away from the tree. Consider your own life: What things are helping or hindering your progress to the tree of eternal life?

In the world we live in, I think that verse 33 is becoming ever more important. What do you think?

One of the really cool things we can learn from Lehi's dream is that parents have the right to receive revelation regarding the spiritual welfare of their children (:1-4, 35-36). Lehi could then take action to teach and to testify to his children while not denying their agency (:37-38). Where do you see the different members of your own family in Lehi's dream, and what elements of the dream would help them move toward the tree or to stay there?

7

Day 11, 1 Nephi 9:1-10:10

Nephi made two sets of plates containing his record. What can you learn about these two records from 1 Nephi 9:1-4, and footnote 2a?

In 1 Nephi 9:5-6 we get Nephi's reason for why he made two sets of plates. Notice the word "all" in verse 6.

Here is a timeline that will help us better understand God's omniscient knowledge. Lehi left Jerusalem in 600 B.C. Nephi is commanded to make his first record in 589 B.C. (1 Nephi 19:1). He is commanded to make his second record between 569-559 B.C. (2 Nephi 5:29-33). Mormon includes the small plates with the large plates in 385 A.D. (The Words of Mormon 1:3-7). Then Joseph Smith loses the 116 pages which contained information from the large plates (D&C 3). At the end of the translation process Joseph was informed about the small plates which contained greater material and covered the same time frame as that which was lost (D&C 10:38-45). In what ways does this timeline confirm what Nephi said about the Lord in 1 Nephi 9:6?

What are some of the different prophecies Nephi said that Lehi made in 1 Nephi 10:1-10? Which of those have come to pass?

From what we have seen in today's section, why can we trust the Lord and His prophets?

Day 12, 1 Nephi 10:11-11:11

Yesterday, Lehi made several prophecies about Jerusalem and Jesus Christ. Today, in 1 Nephi 10:11-14, Lehi continues to prophesy about the scattering and gathering of Israel. Has Lehi prophesied about our time yet?

Nephi wants to see and hear what his father did and we want a greater increase of revelation in our own life. Search 1 Nephi 10:17-11:11 for all the things that helped Nephi and would also help us receive more revelation. There are a few major themes that are repeated several times, but there are also a couple of others that are only mentioned once or even just hinted at, so read carefully. Which one of the things you found has helped you the most in getting revelation?

In 1 Nephi 10:17-11:11 we are also given an incredible amount of information about the Holy Ghost. What did you learn about him?

Notice that once you receive a witness, you are expected to bear it (11:7).

Day 13, 1 Nephi 11:12-30

Pay attention to how often Nephi is told to "look" and he "looked." Elder David A. Bednar gives an interesting thought about this: "In chapters 11 through 14 the Holy Ghost assisted Nephi in learning about the nature and meaning of his father's vision. Interestingly, 13 times in these chapters the Spirit of the Lord directed Nephi to 'look' as a fundamental feature of the learning process. Nephi repeatedly was counseled to look, and because he was quick to observe, he beheld the tree of life (1 Nephi 11:8); the mother of the Savior (1 Nephi 11:20); the rod of iron (1 Nephi 11:25); and the Lamb of God, the Son of the Eternal Father (1 Nephi 11:21). I have described only a few of the spiritually significant things Nephi saw. You may want to study these chapters in greater depth and learn from and about Nephi's learning. As you study and ponder, please keep in mind that Nephi would not have seen what he desired to see, he would not have known what he needed to know, and he could not have done what he ultimately needed to do if he had not been quick to observe. Brothers and sisters, that same truth applies to you and to me!" ("Quick to Observe" BYU Speeches, 10 May 2005, 4).

Nephi was asked if he knew the "condescension of God." Condescension means the voluntary descent from a position of rank or dignity. In today's verses we will see both the condescension of God the Father (:17-23) to have a mortal son and God the Son (:24-30) who lived among mortals. What do you find amazing about this idea of the condescension of Gods for their people because they love them?

Day 14, 1 Nephi 11:31-12:10

We will continue to discuss the condescension of Jesus. His voluntary descent from heaven to live among us. In 1 Nephi 11:31-33, notice the difference between what He does for others versus what happens to Him. The challenge in following the Savior is that we are to treat others better than they treat us. Why do you think this is difficult? How can His example help us?

Throughout Nephi's vision we have received the interpretation of what the tree, the fruit, and the iron rod mean. In 1 Nephi 11:34-36 we learn about the "great and spacious building." What is it? Who is in it? What will happen to it? Why do you think there are members of the house of Israel in this building fighting against the twelve apostles of the Lamb (:35)? What kinds of things are causing people to fight against the apostles? How do we know if we are clinging to their words or cringing at their words?

1 Nephi 12:1-10 is a brief summary of the Book of Mormon up to the appearing of Christ.

Day 15, 1 Nephi 12:11-13:9

Spoiler alert: Today's section continues with a prophecy about what will happen to the Book of Mormon people after the Savior appears to them (12:11-15, 19-23). How do you think Nephi felt as he was shown what would happen?

How does a person become clean and pure according to 1 Nephi 12:7?

In 1 Nephi 12:16-18, we are told the interpretation for three of the key features of the tree of life vision. Which of these three do you find most interesting? Knowing these interpretations adds layers of depth and understanding to 1 Nephi 8.

After seeing the destruction and apostasy of his own people, Nephi is shown the apostasy of many nations by the Church of the Devil. This is not any one specific church, but a combination of ideas, philosophies, and practices that corrupt and destroy the opportunity for eternal life. As you read 1 Nephi 13:1-9 look for what the desires of this church are.

Day 16, 1 Nephi 13:10-27

Nephi continues to write his unfolding vision about the rediscovery and founding of America. As you read verses 10-19 what evidence do you see that God was involved with the framing of a free country where the restoration of the gospel could happen?

"This great American nation the Almighty raised up by the power of his omnipotent hand, that it might be possible in the latter days for the kingdom of God to be established in the earth. If the Lord had not prepared the way by laying the foundations of this glorious nation, it would have been impossible (under the stringent laws and bigotry of the monarchical governments of the world) to have laid the foundations for the coming of his great kingdom. The Lord has done this" (Joseph F. Smith. Gospel Doctrine, 5th ed. [1939], 409).

The next increment in Nephi's vision is about a book: the Bible. What does the angel teach Nephi about the Bible in verses 20-27?

Day 17, 1 Nephi 13:28-38

If you were Satan and you could destroy any part of the tree of life vision, except the tree and its fruit, what would it be? As you read today's section you may want to mark the phrase "plain and precious."

Notice what happens as people cling to a rod of iron that has parts missing, they are still on the path, but progress is slow and there is some tripping.

I know of nothing that has caused more people to struggle than the desaturation of the word of God that occurred throughout the apostasy and the accompanying infusion of worldly philosophies and theories in its place.

Day 18, 1 Nephi 13:39-14:7

Take a pencil and draw a line, then erase parts of it. This represents the rod of iron after the apostasy. Now read 1 Nephi 13:39-41 and look for what the Lord does to fix it. As you read, fill in some of the gaps that you made.

What does 1 Nephi 13:40 promise that the "last records," or the latter-day records, will do for the "first" or the Bible?

What is the purpose of all of these records coming together according to 1 Nephi 13:42-14:1-7? In what ways has he manifest himself to you lately? Are the scriptures saving or destroying you?

Day 19, 1 Nephi 14:8-30

In the Tree of Life vision there are two major gathering places: the tree and the great and spacious building. As you read verses 9-17, look for what you can discover about these two great gathering centers. Where can they be found? Which one is larger? What does verse 14 teach you about why one of these can't be destroyed?

In verses 18-30 we learn that Lehi and Nephi were not the only ones who have seen this same vision. Who else has seen it and what do we learn about what they wrote concerning it? What does this teach us about when to write sacred experiences, when not to, and when to share or not share what we have experienced?

Day 20, 1 Nephi 15:1-20

After Nephi returns from beholding the vision, he finds Laman and Lemuel disputing over the words of Lehi. This experience is so real. We do not live our lives in spiritual euphoria but in the realities of daily life. We are on different spiritual levels. As you read verses 1-11, look for what would help or hinder spiritual understanding and insight. Which of those things mentioned has been the greatest help and which has been the greatest hindrance to you personally?

Verses 12-20 are a wonderful summary about the history and future of the Jews and Gentiles. Notice that whichever group has the gospel also has a responsibility to share it with those who don't. Please look and pray for opportunities to help others receive "strength and nourishment from the true vine" (:15).

Day 21, 1 Nephi 15:21-36

As Nephi explains to his brothers what the iron rod means, he shares some of the promises that come from scripture study and righteous living in verse 24. What evidence do you have in your own life that those promises are real and not just wasted words?

Next, Nephi explains to his brothers about the judgment of the Lord in dividing the righteous from the wicked. In verses 33-36, look for why God can't just bring the filthy into his kingdom.

What filthy thought, feeling, or action has God been trying to get you to give up lately so that He can bring you into His kingdom?

Day 22, 1 Nephi 16:1-16

What additional insights can the following quote give us about verses 1-5? "The prophet tells us what we need to know, not always what we want to know. ... Or, to put it in another prophet's words, 'Hit pigeons flutter.'" (Ezra Taft Benson. Fourteen Fundamentals in Following the Prophet. BYU

Devotional 1980). How should we respond when something cuts us to our center?

I will never forget my experience as a missionary teaching Henry Jones. When he read verse 7 he said, "You mean Nephi got the hook up? Ah, man that's great." Then he read verse 8 and said, "I knew that marriage was a commandment."

Verses 9-16 are a great example of what the gospel does for a person's life. There is still the same travel, work, and journey, but you should also be led to find "the more fertile parts of the wilderness" (:16). Look for how God is leading you to the more fertile parts of your life today.

Day 23, 1 Nephi 16:17-39

As we journey through life, things will inevitably go wrong. In today's section, we will read about the breaking of Nephi's bow and the death of Ishmael. What can we learn about overcoming challenges by observing the different members of these families?

Who did you most act like the last time you faced a problem? In what ways might you act differently today as you encounter problems and complications? Which problem do you think was bigger, Nephi's broken bow or his family's broken faith and hope? What does verse 23 teach you about overcoming challenges?

In verse 34 we learn that the place where Ishmael is buried is called "Nahom." Much has been written by LDS scholars about this name because it appears that the discovery of some altars may provide archeological evidence that such a place existed. A quick Google search for "Nahom in the Book of Mormon" will provide you with several articles, many in favor and some opposed.

Day 24, 1 Nephi 17:1-16

In verses 1-6, Nephi describes the travel through the wilderness that his family experienced. Then in verse 3, Nephi teaches us a lesson that he thinks we should all learn by using the phrase "thus we see." So what's the lesson?

What does the word "prepared" in verses 3 and 6 add to our understanding about Nephi's journey, our lives, and God's help?

The Lord prepared the land of Bountiful as a place of respite and a launching pad for the next part of their journey. In our own lives, God desires us to progress, moving us forward and upward. For Nephi it is the Promised Land, for us it is the attainment of the Celestial Kingdom by becoming celestial. In verses 7-16, look at the partnership that exists between Nephi and God. What does each partner in this cosmic dance of progression do to help with the journey to the Promised Land? How is this the same with us?

Day 25, 1 Nephi 17:17-30

God really does believe that he can improve us, so He asks us to do challenging things often and, sometimes, even incredibly hard things. Nephi was asked to build a boat to transport his family to the Promised Land. What has the Lord asked you to do to transport your family to a promised kingdom? In what ways is Nephi's ship similar to temples?

Nephi responded to the Lord's challenge with hope, faith, and courage. Notice how his brothers responded to the Lord's challenge and Nephi's response in verses 17-22. Which comment do you think hurt Nephi the most?

There are still Lamans and Lemuels today that mock what people of faith do and believe. They would have us abandon the construction of ships and a way of living that would transport us and our families to eternal lands of promise, and in their place they would offer us things of momentary pleasure with no lasting value. We must remember 1 Nephi 8:33 when their mocking jeers and sharp worded barbs bite.

In verses 23-30, look for how Nephi used the scriptures to find similarities to his own life. What good are the scriptures and their stories unless we can use the principles that they teach to help us in our own lives? Nephi used the story of Moses. Similarly, how have you used the story of Nephi to bolster your faith, hope, and courage in the last few days? Then, as you share, others will use your stories and example to assist them. That is how the cycle continues.

Day 26, 1 Nephi 17:31-47

In verses 31-38, Nephi speaks of the destruction that Israel was asked to perform when they returned from Egypt. The idea of destruction can be confusing unless you understand the concept of "ripe in iniquity" (:36). Corruption had reached a point that children being born into those families no longer possessed the possibility of choosing goodness. For examples of this corruption see Leviticus 18, and 20. With a knowledge of the Spirit World we can also see how God's destruction stops further corruption, while allowing for opportunity to be instructed (D&C 138:32-37). There are other examples of God's willingness to destroy: the flood, the Nephites, and the second coming of Christ. So from what we have learned, how can destruction also be an act of kindness, mercy, and justice?

Nephi also speaks of the Lord correcting the Children of Israel. On one such occasion, venomous snakes were allowed to bite them, but if they looked to a brass serpent which Moses made, they would be saved. Verse 41 tells us why many didn't look and live. Will you find ways today to look to the Savior for help?

President Boyd K. Packer once said this about verse 45: "Perhaps the single greatest thing I learned from reading the Book of Mormon is that the voice of the Spirit comes as a feeling rather than a sound. You will learn, as I have learned, to 'listen' for that voice that is felt rather than heard. Nephi scolded his older brothers, saying, 'Ye have seen an angel, and he spake unto you; yea, ye have heard his voice from time to time; and he hath spoken unto you in a still small voice, but ye were past feeling, that ye could not feel his words.' Some critics have said that these verses are in error because you hear words; you do not feel them. But if you know anything at all about spiritual communication, you know that the best word to describe what takes place is the word feeling." ("Counsel to Youth." Ensign, Oct 2011. p. 19).

Day 27, 1 Nephi 17:48-18:4

For a long time, I have loved the words of verses 48-51. They have often helped motivate me to do what the Lord has asked me to do, especially when I replace the last few words, "build a ship" (:51), with my own like: raise a family, share my testimony, serve a mission, really repent, gain an education, hold family prayer, pay my tithing, honor my covenants, repent and visit with my Bishop, or any other variety of things. Do you believe, like Nephi, in God's power and willingness to help you with things?

In verses 52-55, God shocks Laman and Lemuel into obedience. Why do you think He doesn't do this more with people? What other means does God use to get our attention? When have you had a shocking experience or wakeup call from the Lord and His prophets? Why do you think the effects of this experience weren't lasting for Laman and Lemuel?

I am intrigued by the words "manner" and "oft" (18:2-3). What lessons and insights come to your mind about your life when you think about these words?

Day 28, 1 Nephi 18:5-20

Notice in verse 9 that it was the rudeness that caused the problem and not dancing and merry-making. How we do things is sometimes as important as what we do and why. How can you tell if something you do is rude or inappropriate to the Lord?

As you read the rest of the story, look for what effect Laman and Lemuel's sins had on the other people in the story. When other people's choices cause us pain, sorrow, and tears, how can we do what Nephi did in verse 16?

When we make poor choices and sin against God, storms and struggles will eventually come upon us. Why do you think it took Laman and Lemuel so long to repent? Why do we sometimes wait until we are almost swallowed up before we repent (:20)? Today, if you do something that is rudeness before the Lord, will you repent quicker, so that you may resume your journey to the Promised Land?

Day 29, 1 Nephi 18:21-19:6

Yesterday, we left the family on the brink of destruction, and Nephi had just had his cords loosed. In 1 Nephi 18:21-22, the things that Nephi does to regain control of their lives, ship, and journey are mentioned. Why do you think Nephi establishes his direction before calming the storm? When he does pray, there is a "great calm" (:22). When was the last time prayer brought you a great calm?

At the end of today's section Nephi describes his role in making multiple sets of plates (19:1-6). The smaller plates contain the things he considered to be "more sacred" (19:5). If sacred experiences are not recorded and treasured, they are dimmed and even forgotten in time. How do you record and treasure your sacred experiences?

Nephi also admits his human weakness in making these plates and recording sacred things (19:6). Many critics search for any little thing they can find to disprove the truth claims of the Book of Mormon. One of the things they look for is called anachronism, or things that are mentioned that shouldn't be. A favorite among critics is the mention of "horse" as one of the animals found in the Promised Land (18:25). "Ah ha," the critic says, "we finally have him. Joseph Smith is an idiot. Everyone knows that horses arrived with the Spaniards." This is true, and yet there is also evidence that there were ancient horses in the Americas, but many believed that they were extinct by the time the Nephites arrived. There is also some evidence, though not as much as we would like, that these animals were still around at the time of their arrival. This is a good question, for which we don't have a perfect answer yet.

Another favorite argument of the critics is the weight of the golden plates. Given the described dimensions of height, length, and width would be about 300 pounds if made of pure gold. This is not, however, what the text says. Nephi reports on what metals he found in the Promised Land in 1 Nephi 18:25, and then declares that with those metals he made "plates of ore" (19:1). We often miss that the plates were made up of various metals because of an inserted chapter heading. The reported weight of 50-60 pounds by the witnesses and Martin Harris, who actually hefted them, are accurate when considering an amalgamated metal instead of solid gold.

Day 30, 1 Nephi 19:7-24

Verse 7 contains quite a powerful image. What are some things that are of "great worth...to...[your] body and soul" that you have seen others trample and set at nought? What sacred things does God want you to be more careful with in the future?

In verses 8-10, we are given a list of things that Christ "suffered" through and "yielded" to. Look for why he allowed those things to happen to himself. In what ways is this answer incredible to you?

In verses 11-12, look for how the creation responded when the blood of its creator fell upon it.

Look for what Nephi says about the House of Israel and eventually to the House of Israel in verses 13-21.

Verse 23 is often quoted in relation to scripture study. In what ways has Nephi's formula for studying the scriptures helped you?

Day 31, 1 Nephi 20:1-22

Many people have a living fear of reading Isaiah, but we don't need to. One thing that makes him difficult to read is, that among other things, he is a poet; he wrote in parallelism. This means he only says half as much as you think he does; he repeats the same idea multiple times so that we don't miss it. Read one verse at a time and look for him repeating the same idea, but with different words. It also helps if you read him out loud.

Here is a brief summary of the chapter: "The Lord invites disobedient Israel (:1-8) to repent and return from the wicked ways of the world (:9-17) so they can have peace (:18-22)." Look for your favorite line from each of those sections.

Can you see the basic themes of the chapter as you read?

Day 32, 1 Nephi 21:1-21

In verses 1-7, we hear a servant of the Lord calling for the lost to return, and then we learn some things as God speaks to his discouraged servant. Those who are called to be the Lord's servants, include Christ, prophets, and anyone else who ever serves. Which line in these verses do you relate to most?

Verses 8-13 deal with first the spiritual and then the physical gathering that will take place in the last days and the comfort and mercy that will come.

Before people are gathered and healed, they will have moments when they feel that God has forsaken them (:14). The Lord makes promises that "He does not, indeed he cannot forget his people" (:15-16). Why is that so important to know, and when have you felt that it is true?

In verses 17-21 we are told that there will be so many gathered, that the promised lands won't be enough.

Day 33, 1 Nephi 21:22-22:10

1 Nephi 21:22-23 are explained by Nephi to his brothers in 1 Nephi 22:1-10. How well are you fulfilling your role as a nursing mother and father to those in spiritual need? What faces, names, and actions come to your mind as you read these words?

If you have ever tried to recover a hotdog from a dog, then you will understand 1 Nephi 21:24-25. Now imagine what a miracle it would be if the prey of a lion or a bear escaped. What a miracle it would be if even sin and death had to deliver up their prey. You and I know people, even children, that are in situations and places where it seems almost impossible for their delivery. Trust the "Savior," trust the "Redeemer," trust in "the Mighty One of Jacob" (:21:26). When have you seen the redemption of one who you thought was lost?

Day 34, 1 Nephi 22:11-31

Today's whole section speaks about the current and coming gathering of both the righteous and the wicked in many different ways. When do you gather with the righteous and when do you gather with the wicked?

What is one reason the Lord gives for justifying the destruction of the wicked at the second coming in verses 16-17?

Amputation is a very aggressive treatment. In verses 19-21, look for who is cut off and why?

We know that Satan will be bound during the millennium. In verse 26, we learn how this will happen. Satan or yourself will be bound today; from what you learned how will you make sure it is him?

Day 35, 2 Nephi 1:1-12

1 Nephi chapter 1 ended with a discussion about tender mercies of the Lord. 2 Nephi 1:1-3 starts with a discussion about the mercies of the Lord. In what ways have you seen the mercy of the Lord in your life this year?

Lehi had a vision of the destruction of Jerusalem (:4). This spiritual witness about the destruction of Jerusalem came about 300 years before they received confirming physical evidence in the discovery of the people of

Zarahemla, the descendants of Mulek, son of Zedekiah (Omni 1:14-17). Why do you think the Lord provided the spiritual witness before producing the physical proof? Does he do this with our lives as well?

From verses 5-12, what can we learn about the Promised Land that Lehi and Nephi's family inherited? Who else may come to this land, and what are the conditions upon which they are led and allowed to prosper?

Day 36, 2 Nephi 1:13-29

In today's section, Lehi delivers his last bit of counsel to Laman, Lemuel, Sam, and the sons of Ishmael. You are probably familiar with this type of talk. You might have received it in your youth or even delivered it as a parent. Here are some questions to consider:

After reading the section, how would you summarize this talk into one sentence?

What is a phrase Lehi used that you believe may have stuck out to his children?

What examples of awaking from "the sleep of hell" have you seen in your life?

In verse 21, Lehi tells his sons to "be men." What can we learn from the surrounding verses about Lehi's expectations for manhood? Who do you know that qualifies to be a man according to Lehi's definition?

In verse 24, Lehi tells his sons that Nephi has "kept the commandments from the time that we left Jerusalem." What might that be implying about Nephi's past? How can that bit of knowledge be helpful or hopeful?

Day 37, 2 Nephi 1:30-2:10

Of all of the blessings and counsel offered before father Lehi departs, the smallest is given to Zoram (1:30-32). This however does not mean that it is not significant. Notice how Zoram's life impacted others. Can the things said of Zoram also be said of you?

As Lehi begins talking with Jacob, he mentions the many afflictions and sorrows that have been his (2:1). Lehi then tells Jacob that the greatness of

God is found in his ability not to remove affliction, sorrow, and pain, but to be able to consecrate/make holy our afflictions for our benefit (2:2). A God that does not stop our worst moments, but is able to change them, is truly powerful. When have you felt your afflictions, sorrows, or pain transformed into a blessing or benefit? What current afflictions are you waiting on Him to transform?

Perhaps the greatest evidence of God's power to transform affliction to gain is the process of redeeming us from our sins. This process is described very well in 2 Nephi 2:3-10. Is there anything else in those verses that you feel is worth looking at closer?

Day 38, 2 Nephi 2:11-21

Rather than give you some questions today, I want to give you a challenge. The verses in today's section are so rich in content that they are constantly allowing for new insights and discoveries. Read a verse or a couple of verses and then stop and write down any thoughts, impressions, or questions you have.

Day 39, 2 Nephi 2:22-3:5

On a piece of paper make three columns. Label the first "Before the Fall," the second "After the Fall," and the third "Through the Atonement." As you read 2 Nephi 2:22-25, you will be able to fill in the first and second columns, and with a little pondering you can then fill in the third. Then write down what you learned.

In 2 Nephi 2:26-30, what choice are we told that we have because Christ performed the Atonement? Why wasn't that a choice before Christ performed the Atonement?

2 Nephi 3:1-5 is Lehi's parting counsel to his son Joseph and the beginning of a prophecy made by another Joseph who was sold into Egypt.

Day 40, 2 Nephi 3:6-25

Today Lehi quotes from a prophecy by Joseph, who was sold into Egypt. This prophecy was recorded on the Brass Plates and is also found in JST Genesis 50:24-38. In this brief section there are more than 40 prophecies about Joseph Smith, Moses, and the Book of Mormon. Be careful: You can get tripped up on some of the pronouns.

How do you think Joseph and Oliver felt when they translated these words? Which of these prophecies still makes your jaw drop?

What are the prophecies and promises about the Book of Mormon and the Bible in verse 12? Which of those do you feel is most needed in our world today? How have any of these prophecies been fulfilled in your own life?

Day 41, 2 Nephi 4:1-27

What principles can we learn about being parents and grandparents from verses 3-11?

Nephi describes his feelings toward the scriptures and gospel study in verses 15-16 by using the words "delighteth" and "pondereth." What words would you use to describe your feelings?

Verses 17-27 are a part of what is commonly called Nephi's psalm. As you read, look for what Nephi says about himself and what he says about God. Why do you think it is good to know that prophets have felt that way before?

Day 42, 2 Nephi 4:28-5:9

Today Nephi continues his psalm. In 2 Nephi 4:28-35, look for how Nephi, a great man, uses his belief in the Atonement to make him even better. What changes does he want to happen within him? What does he pray for? What commitments and promises does he make?

How can you use the teaching found in 2 Nephi 4:34 today?

In 2 Nephi 5:1-9, we learn that changing your geographical location doesn't change people much when compared to the Atonement. The family of Lehi have obtained the Promised Land, but not the qualities of love at home. Look for what made family life hard. The Lord will warn you of dangers to your family just as he did Nephi (:5). What small but subtle change or effort does the Lord want you to make to help your family?

Day 43, 2 Nephi 5:10-27

In verse 27, Nephi says "we lived after the manner of happiness." Search verses 11-18 for which things they were doing that have also brought you happiness.

Verses 19-25 often cause confusion and questions if they are not read correctly. The "curse" mentioned in these verses is not dark skin; the curse, as is mentioned in verse 20, is being "cut off from the presence of the Lord." You may want to read these verses and mentally make that change. Once you have done that you will also be able to see that the mark of dark skin served a different purpose for a limited time.

There is racism in the Book of Mormon, and thank goodness for that, because there is racism in our world. The Book of Mormon is the only religious text that really engages with this problem. As you continue to read this year, watch for how the Lord continually asks whichever race that is righteous at the time to reach out with love to the other. The Book of Mormon contains principles that, if applied, will help us and others overcome racism.

Day 44, 2 Nephi 5:28-6:5

In 2 Nephi 5:28-34, Nephi is asked by the Lord to make a second record of their travels, which is what we have been reading. I don't know if I would have responded with obedience the way that Nephi does to what would have appeared to be a redundant commandment. What about you?

In chapter 6, we are introduced to the voice of Jacob, the prophet Nephi's younger brother, who has been anointed to be a teacher. What can we learn about teaching the gospel from Jacob's example as you carefully consider and read verses 1-5?

Day 45, 2 Nephi 6:8-7:11

This is the third time that content of 2 Nephi 6:6-7 has been referred to or commented on in the Book of Mormon. There must be something significant here. In his explanation, Jacob gives a sweeping view of the history of the Jews and Gentiles (6:8-18). These are things that have and will happen. What is left is for us to decide what role we will play.

In 2 Nephi 6:13, we learn that a distinguishing feature of the people of the Lord is that they "wait for him." Nothing builds our patience and tests our faith more than having to wait for the promised deliverance and redemption. In what ways has waiting on the Lord paid off in your life? What promises of the Lord are you still waiting for?

To help us understand the Lord's commitment to his people, Jacob quotes Isaiah as he compares our relationship to the Lord to an unfaithful spouse in marriage. Notice what the Lord says about not leaving us and His constant power to save us (7:1-3). How does this example help us understand that a covenant is more like a powerful love story than a business contract?

In 2 Nephi 7:4-9, we see the Savior's commitment to accomplish what he promised us he would.

2 Nephi 7:10-11 promises that we will have the light of the Lord so long as we do not "walk in the light of your own fire."

Day 46, 2 Nephi 8

To help us understand that the Savior desires to redeem His covenant people and has the power to do so, we get 2 Nephi 8, or Jacob quoting Isaiah 51. Look for what promises the Lord makes to those who hearken to the Lord and the prophets and awaken from their sins. As you read, consider which of those is the hardest to do: listening and acting, looking to and following examples, or awaking from sins?

When was a time you felt the Lord trying to keep His covenant to save you?

After showing us that He desires to save us, the Lord invites the Jews and us to make the changes that will allow for that salvation (:17, 24-25). The "arise" and "sit down" references make more sense if we know that the Lord is asking us to move and change our lives, and not just practice calisthenics. What does the Lord want you to arise and shake off from your life? What does He want you to put on that is beautiful, and where does He want you to settle?

Day 47, 2 Nephi 9:1-14

What do verses 5-9 say about why there had to be an Atonement, and what would happen to us if there was no Atonement?

We have now learned what would happen to us without an Atonement. Now in verses 10-14, it will tell us about what will happen to us because there is an Atonement.

Which of the following phrases best describes how you feel about what you have learned today: "O the wisdom of God, his mercy and grace" (:8), "O how great the goodness of our God" (:10), or "O how great the plan of our God" (:13)?

Day 48, 2 Nephi 9:15-38

Yesterday we learned about the Atonement. Today we will continue with another result of the Atonement, being that each person must experience judgment (:15-19).

What do verses 20-22 say about why Christ is capable and qualified to issue judgment? Why do you think it is important for us to feel comfortable and confident in Christ's abilities as our Judge?

In verses 23-27, we learn about the law that Christ uses to judge and about the role of the Atonement when people who lack awareness of the law act as judges.

Now, with an understanding of judgment and confidence in our Judge, we are warned of things that we may misjudge in our own life in verses 28-38. Which "wo" may be the most important for you to heed at this time in your life?

Day 49, 2 Nephi 9:39-53

In verses 39-41, we are counseled to "remember" several things. Why do you feel that it is important that we remember these different things? What difference has it made when you have or haven't remembered those things?

Next, we are counseled in verses 42-46 to "cast these things away," "shake off," and "turn away" from several things. How can wisdom, pride, riches, and sin hide "that happiness which is prepared for the saints" (:43)?

Which invitation mentioned in verses 50-53 do you find most appealing? What other words, phrases, and ways can you think of to invite people to come and partake of the Atonement of Jesus Chris

Day 50, 2 Nephi 9:54-10:17

In 2 Nephi 9:54, Jacob stops this already wonderful talk that he has been giving to the people of Nephi since chapter 6 to say that he will continue the rest of it the next day. As part of that next day sermon, Jacob reveals what an angel taught him about Christ during the night (10:1-5). This is the first recorded use of the title "Christ" in the scriptures.

One of the major things that Jacob reveals about Christ is that regardless of how far or how long people have been scattered and lost, He wants them to return and believe (10:2, 7-9). Why do you think it is important to know that when it comes to salvation, we are the ones who limit ourselves and not our Redeemer?

What promises have been made about land and people in 2 Nephi 10:10-17?

Day 51, 2 Nephi 10:18-11:8

After a two-day talk, Jacob ends his sermon by offering us a great summary of his sermon in 2 Nephi 10:23-25. In what ways did Jacob's words on the Atonement of Christ "cheer up your hearts"?

How many different ways can you finish the phrase "my soul delighteth . . ."? Nephi does it five times (11:1-8). Which of the things that Nephi delights in do you also delight in?

Members of the Church often tell the folktale of the World War II serviceman who was shot, only to have the bullet stopped by his pocket-sized Book of Mormon. The bullet, of course, stopped at 2 Nephi 11, because not even a bullet can get through Isaiah. Despite what people may think, Isaiah was not thrown into the Book of Mormon to test our faith. Nephi is more careful and calculated with how he uses his plate space than that. Read 2 Nephi 11:2-3 to discover Nephi's true intentions with quoting Isaiah. How might that help us to have a better experience as we study Isaiah for the next several chapters?

Day 52, 2 Nephi 12

Remember that Isaiah uses parallelism to explain his ideas, so he says everything twice. Slow down and don't overthink it.

In verses 1-5, Isaiah sees people gathering to the temples in the last days. Look for the results of this temple gathering. Which of these have you noticed in your own life?

After mentioning some really incredible blessings for temple worship, Isaiah then outlines several things that keep us from qualifying for these blessings in verses 6-9.

Verses 10-22 speak of the second coming of Christ. In that day, notice what is brought down, or humbled, and what is exalted, or raised up.

Day 53, 2 Nephi 13-14

In 2 Nephi 13:1-12, we see verses that have dual meaning. These verses describe the results of wicked behavior upon Isaiah's Kingdom of Judah, as well as modern Israel. Look for what happens to leadership and compassion when wickedness is selected over righteousness. 2 Nephi 13:8 points out that it is not only what we do wrong that hurts us, but also what we say.

In 2 Nephi 13:13-15, the Lord declares that He will pass judgment for the mistreatment of the poor. One of the reasons that the poor are left uncared for is because of the ancient and modern obsession with fashion and style, so that there is nothing left for the poor (:13:16-24). In those same verses, look for how well Isaiah describes the problem of being fashion-obsessed, as well as the accompanying consequences.

Some have thought that 2 Nephi 14:1 is a reference to polygamy being reinstated. The shortage of men is a result of 2 Nephi 13:25-26. This cannot be polygamy, as was sometimes practiced by the Church, because the women fend for themselves and are not supported by the men.

2 Nephi 14:2-6 deals with the women who survive the judgment of the last chapter. They will be called holy (:3) after they are washed (:4) and their righteous influence will be so great that every house will become as a temple (:5-6). What does this teach us about the impact a woman of the Lord can make versus a woman of the world?

Day 54, 2 Nephi 15

The song of the vineyard in verses 1-7 contains several wonderful analogies between the how Lord treats the vineyard and how he treats the house of Israel. What evidence of justice and mercy did you see?

The term "wo," which is used seven times in the next few verses, is associated with the anguish and distress of those who receive the judgment of the Lord. Following is a brief summary of each:

Verses 8-10 speaks out against the improper use of land.
Verses 11-17 contains the prophetic word on the manner in which those of the world improperly and with evil intent eat, drink, and make merry.
Verses 18-19 is directed against those who are wicked and mock God and his divine plan.
Verse 20 speaks against liars and those who fight against the things of God.
Verse 21 deals with conceited individuals who believe themselves to be wise.
Verses 22-23 accuses those who give bribes and belittle the righteous.

Which woes do you feel are in abundance in our world today?

Verses 25-30 describe how the Lord in a wicked world will reach out his hand to save all that he can by raising up his ensign/church and calling to all nations by his missionary servants and the Holy Ghost to be gathered to safety. Why do you think it is important to know that the Lord continually seeks to reclaim those who are engaged in wicked practices?

Day 55, 2 Nephi 16-17

In 2 Nephi 16:1-5, Isaiah sees an angel and the Lord. Isaiah feels unworthy to be in the Lord's presence because of sins that he has committed with his mouth. What unrepented sins would we be aware of if we were to come into the presence of the Lord?

In 2 Nephi 16:6-7, Isaiah has his sins forgiven by having a hot coal from the altar placed on his mouth. Ouch. The coal came from the altar upon which sacrifices were offered, thus the coal represents the Atonement of Christ being laid upon Isaiah's sin. How have you experienced the same purging as Isaiah? On what things in your life do you need to place the Atonement?

After being cleansed, Isaiah is ready and willing to accept a difficult mission call that will result in few converts and his eventual death (16:8-13). How does experiencing the Atonement in our own lives help to make us willing to serve the Lord and others?

2 Nephi 17 contains an account of a time when the Kingdom of Judah was being threatened by Syria and Israel. In 2 Nephi 17:1-9, the Lord has the prophet Isaiah proclaim to Ahaz, the King of Judah, that Syria and Israel will be destroyed. For assurance of this prophecy, the Lord promised a sign of a virgin bearing a son (7:14). This prophecy was fulfilled twice. Once, with the birth of Isaiah's son through his righteous and virtuous wife, and the second through Mary and Jesus Christ. The name "Immanuel" means "God with us." Please ponder about times when you have felt the meaning of that name in your own life. Finally in 2 Nephi 17:17-25, Isaiah tells of the coming invasion of Assyria against Judah.

Day 56, 2 Nephi 18

In verses 1-4, we see the first fulfillment of the prophecy made yesterday about a virgin bearing a son; the second will come with the birth of Christ. Isaiah and his wife, the prophetess, will have a son, Maher-shalal-hash-baz. Before he is old enough to talk, Syria and Israel—with their capitals Damascus and Samaria—will be destroyed and they will no longer threaten the kingdom of Judah.

In verse 18 we learn that Isaiah's sons are to be signs to the people. Both of their names teach valuable lessons. Maher-shalal-hash-baz means destruction is imminent (18:1a), and Shearjashub means a remnant shall return (Isaiah 7:3a). Thus, any time people would meet Isaiah's sons, they would know that the Babylonian destruction will one day come and that a remnant of those carried away would also return.

Verses 5-16 speak about how the people have rejected trusting in Jehovah and instead put their trust in making alliances with the King of Assyria to deliver them from their current problems with Israel and Syria. This rejection is described as the people rejecting the soft rolling waters of Shiloah, a little stream near the Temple Mount, for the great but unpredictable and dangerous Euphrates, a river in Assyria known for its flooding. After Assyria destroyed Judah's enemies, it turned on Judah and almost annihilated them. Why do you think people are prone to reject the soft but steady safety and counsel of Jesus Christ and seek other solutions?

In verses 17-22, we learn that our God is a master of hide and seek. Why do you think he stays hidden unless we look and then wait for him? We could all take the advice that President Thomas S. Monson gave to a downcast and overwhelmed leader: "It is better to look up" (Carl B. Cook. Ensign, Nov 2011).

Day 57, 2 Nephi 19-20:4

Yesterday we learned that those who look to the earth or man for answers will receive darkness and dimness. Following the destruction of the kingdom of Israel by Assyria and the kingdom of Judah by Babylon, a long darkness dwelled upon the promised land, but Isaiah promised a day of light when he prophesied of Christ's coming (19:1-2).

In 2 Nephi 19:3-7, we find one of Isaiah's most well-known prophesies about the coming Messiah. What are the names that will be given to him? These names are not just titles, but also calls to action. Consider the following questions for each name: How did He, how does He, and how will He fulfill each of these names and titles for us collectively and to you individually?

2 Nephi 19:8-20:4 contains a warning of destruction to the northern 10 tribes of Israel, as well as to modern day Israel for their wicked deed described in 2 Nephi 19:14-17. Despite the rebellion and rejection of Christ, He still stand with "his hand stretched out still" to save or to destroy (19:12, 17, 21, 20:4). How will use your agency today to reach out for salvation?

Day 58, 2 Nephi 20:5-34

In verses 5-11, the Lord says he used the Assyrian King and army to punish disobedient and wicked nations like ancient Israel had become. This whole idea can be summarized by looking at D&C 117:6.

After the Lord used Assyria to destroy Israel, He then destroyed Assyria like He will do with all wicked and filthy things at his coming (:12-19). Notice how the King of Assyria boasts of his pretend strength and power, like an axe in the hand of its master (:13-15). How will you boast of the Lord today rather than of yourself?

In verses 20-27, the Lord promises eventual deliverance to those whom Assyria destroyed if the people will return and "stay upon the Lord" (:20). Check out footnote 20b for a greater understanding of what it means to stay upon the Lord. Also notice how deliverance comes because of the "anointing" (:27). These verses remind me that weekly, hourly, and daily I don't stay upon the Lord or his Atonement like I should. How will you depend upon the Lord today, even this hour?

After destroying the Northern Kingdom of Israel, Assyria then sought to march to Jerusalem in the Southern Kingdom of Judah. Verses 28-32 contains a list of cities that were destroyed by Assyria. Nob is only 1.5 miles from Jerusalem. The people and their King Hezekiah continued to stay upon the Lord with the enemy at their gate. The Lord then cut down Assyria like a tree and saved His people (:33-34, 2 Kings 19:35). He will do a similar work at His second coming.

Day 59, 2 Nephi 21-22

Here are some cross-references that will be very helpful in studying 2 Nephi 21, D&C 113:1-6, JSH 1:40, and Revelations 5:5.

Assyria was cut down yesterday, typifying the destruction of the second coming. Only stumps were left. Today in 2 Nephi 21:1-9, we will see Christ's Millennial reign begin. Look for how he rules and governs. Also look for the conditions that exist during the Millennium.

The image of a new branch growing out of a cut stump continues to be used as Isaiah now jumps from the Millennium back to the restoration. The cut-down trees now represent the age of apostasy; the newly restored church and its leaders are the branch shooting forth (21:10-16). What is taught in this section that helps you want to be faithful and gather others to the ensign before the Savior's Millennial reign?

As far as 2 Nephi 22 goes, we should thank Heavenly Father and Jesus for what they do and praise them for the type of beings that they are.

Day 60, 2 Nephi 23

Verses 1-5 speak of the Lord's army that has been gathered together to defeat the world, or land of wickedness. What do you think is the difference between a person who volunteered for this army and someone who feels that they were drafted?

The destruction of the wicked is a sure promise, but it doesn't have to be the people. It can be the destruction of wicked thoughts, feelings, and actions (:6-22). This whole chapter is a call for us to become a member of the Lord's hosts, one of His sanctified ones, His people (:3-4, 22). What blessings do you think await those who choose to fight this battle every day, versus when they were faced with physical destruction?

When Babylon was destroyed, it was completely wasted. Isaiah promised that it would never be dwelt in or inhabited again (:20).

Day 61, 2 Nephi 24

Verses 1-11 deal with the rest and peace that came when the king of Babylon was no more. When this oppressor of Israel was gone, they could again gather to their home lands. This is also symbolic of the rest and gathering that will one day come to all.

Verses 12-23 are about the fall and destruction of Satan. Notice that he is called Lucifer in verse 12. This is a correct use of the name, for Isaiah is speaking of the pre-existence. Satan is no longer worthy of the name Lucifer; he lost it with the use of his agency. Look up the word Lucifer in the Bible Dictionary to learn more about what this means. This doesn't mean that he was second in command or even the only other option. That idea is most likely a lie that he wants us to believe. In today's section the Lord through his prophet Isaiah will reveal the true intentions and desires of Lucifer in the premortal life. In verses 13-23 look for what Satan wanted and what he will receive. What attitudes led to Satan's ultimate demise? What will happen to us if we possess those same attitudes?

Over the past several chapters, Isaiah has been giving us a great contrast between the Savior and Satan with these prophecies and names. Satan wanted to be above God. He became jealous of Christ and was only thinking of himself. On the other hand, we have "with us is God" (2 Nephi 17:14). Heavenly Father and Jesus Christ want nothing more than for us to be partakers with them of the divine.

Our Heavenly Father and His son Jesus Christ are significantly beyond our comprehension in the perfection of their attributes and character, and yet all they do in their work and glory is seek to raise us up to their level. In contrast, Satan seeks to constantly push us down. Satan never wanted to be equals with God. He wanted to be viewed as better. Thus, in our day-to-day life, do we seek to lift and encourage others or do we look for reasons to view ourselves as better?

Day 62, 2 Nephi 25:1-13

Congratulations on making it through the Isaiah chapters. In verses 1-8, look for what Nephi says about Isaiah, especially verses 7-8. Also look for what he says about plainness.

Nephi mentioned that he was going to include a plain prophecy of his own, part of which he does in verses 9-13. Do you think Nephi would have been able to make such a clear prophecy about the Savior without wrestling with the words of Isaiah? Do you believe that you have wrestled with the scriptures enough to have the Savior and His character plainly manifested to you?

Do you think the following statement is true? Reading Isaiah will make you delight in plainness, which will help you delight in Christ and magnify His holy name.

Day 63, 2 Nephi 25:14-26

In verses 14-22, Nephi continues his prophecy of plainness. Look for what he says regarding Jesus Christ, the Jews, and the role that the Book of Mormon will play to help people believe in Christ. In what ways has the Book of Mormon convinced you that Jesus is the Christ?

There are a couple of different ways the last line of verse 23 can be understood. What do you think that last line means?

What are you doing to accomplish verses 23 and 25 in your own life and home?

According to verses 24-25, how was the Nephite understanding and treatment of the Law of Moses different from the New Testament at the time of Christ?

Day 64, 2 Nephi 25:28-26:13

What do you think of Nephi's powerful ending, warning, and counsel in 2 Nephi 25:28-30?

In 2 Nephi 26:1-13, Nephi sees in vision the future of his people. He sees the rejection of their prophets, their wars, Christ's appearance, and then their final destruction. In 2 Nephi 26:7, look for Nephi's reaction to this vision. What do you think it means when he tells God, "Thy ways are just"?

What does God promise in 2 Nephi 26:3, 11, and 13 in order to be just? In what ways do you see God being just in those verses?

How can knowing that God is just increase your faith in Him and not just your fear?

Day 65, 2 Nephi 26:14-30

In verses 14-19, Nephi sees that the Book of Mormon will come forward in a day of great pride and wickedness. How could a world like that benefit from the Book of Mormon?

Notice that in this world of wickedness, Satan's strategy is to get people to stumble and be bound (:20-22). How have you seen him get others to stumble or be bound? In what ways is Satan seeking to get you to stumble or to be bound?

We can learn many important truths when we contrast Satan's goals and tactics with those of God. Search verses 23-28, marking the words "any" and "all." According to these verses, how does God work? What is the purpose of everything He does? Verse 24 is among the most important on the character of God.

Day 66, 2 Nephi 26:31-27:13

What types of problems and heartache could be solved or cured if the principles in 2 Nephi 26:32-33 could be remembered?

In chapter 27, Nephi again quotes Isaiah. The great apostasy that preceded the Restoration in last days was full of darkness and unfulfilling emptiness, brought on by a rejection of prophets and seers (27:1-5). Do you think personal apostasy could be described the same way and be brought on by the same cause?

The Lord's solution to this predicament is to bring forth the Book of Mormon and restore the gospel keys (27:6). Not all of the plates were translated by Joseph Smith. There remained a portion that was sealed. Look in 2 Nephi 27:7-11 for what we know about what is contained in this sealed portion of the plates.

Notice how these words will one day be read, according to 2 Nephi 27:11. What is keeping us from having that experience with our own scripture study now? How will you get on the rooftops today? When was the last time you felt as though something was being unsealed during your scripture study?

Day 67, 2 Nephi 27:12-35

Verses 12-13 are a prophecy by Isaiah about the Three and Eight Witnesses of the Book of Mormon. What is the advantage of having these witnesses rather than just showing all people the plates?

Verses 14-19 are a prophecy by Isaiah about an experience that occurred in Church history and can be found in JSH 1:63-65. Later Charles Anthon would deny that he endorsed the note and claim that he counseled Martin Harris that Joseph Smith was a fraud. However, Martin went to New York with several personal doubts and when this experience was over he completely committed to the cause of publishing the Book of Mormon, even at the loss of some of his farm.

Verses 20-35 contain many of the problems that faced the world at the time the Book of Mormon was published, as well as the promises that will come to solve these problems. One of my favorites is found in verse 25. The problem is the location of lips and hearts in relation to God. The Book of Mormon is created to draw our hearts and not just our lips closer to God. Have you felt a shift in your heart this year? How has studying the Book of Mormon helped you face challenges and hardships?

Day 68, 2 Nephi 28:1-16

Governments employ experts to detect those who would counterfeit their nation's currency. These experts don't spend their time studying all of the false and fake examples. Instead, they put all of their efforts into a thorough examination of the real things, so that when the fraud is presented they might detect it easier. Because of our study of truth it will be even easier to identify the false traditions, beliefs, philosophies, and logics that are being presented as truths. As you search verses 1-16, identify the counterfeits.

There are many false ideas presented in these verses, but which of the many do you think, if adhered to, would lead to increasing unhappiness?

Why do you think that these false teachings are so appealing?

Day 69, 2 Nephi 28:17-32

Today we will continue with our detection of counterfeits. As you read verses 17-32, look for how many different ways you can complete this sentence: "Satan seeks to grasp us in his power by . . ."

I love that in verse 19 the Lord still wants to stir up to repentance those who are almost hopeless. We worship a God who is worthy of our affection and love.

What does verse 30 teach you about how careful God is with everything that He does?

Day 70, 2 Nephi 29

"Why do Mormons have another Bible?"

In 2 Nephi 29, the word "Gentiles" refers to people who are not of the house of Israel. The word "Jews" refers to people who are of the house of Israel, including Lehi's family and descendants. Read verses 3–6, looking for the reaction some Gentiles would have toward additional scripture.

As you study verses 7-14, find the Lord's purposes for giving scripture in addition to the Bible.

How might 2 Nephi 29 be used to resolve concerns about the Book of Mormon as an additional book of scripture?

How have these verses increased your appreciation for the Book of Mormon?

Day 71, 2 Nephi 30

Read verses 1-2 and then complete this sentence: "Being the Lord's people is not about ancestry but . . ."

What role will the Book of Mormon play prior to the Second Coming and Millennium, according to verses 3-8?

Verses 9-18 describe the conditions of the Millennium. The Lord will slay the wicked, and all of us who are accountable are wicked. Thus, we are allowed to choose how the wicked within us is slain. It can be by the fire of the Second Coming (:10), or by the "rod of his mouth and with the breath of his lips" (:9), which slays our desire to do wickedly. Have you felt a slaying of your wicked desires as you have been studying the scriptures lately?

Day 72, 2 Nephi 31

Nephi said that he would speak about the "doctrine of Christ" (:2). Then, at the end of this chapter, he said that "this is the doctrine of Christ" (:21). As you read this chapter, watch for what the doctrine of Christ is. Then be able to explain each point that you found and its importance.

When Nephi speaks of the baptism of Christ, he does so to teach us several important lessons. Carefully read verses 4-13. Identify as many as these lessons as you can and look for which one will be of use to you today.

What do you think it means when Nephi tells us God "speaketh unto men according to their language, unto their understanding" (:3)? In what ways has this been true with your interactions with revelation?

How well have you done at living verses 19-20 since your baptism?

Day 73, 2 Nephi 32

What do verses 1-6 teach us about receiving direction and guidance? Do you expect to receive direction and guidance today? Why do you think nibbling doesn't produce the same results as feasting?

What principle do you think we are meant to learn about the Spirit from verse 7?

What are some of the subtle lessons about prayer that we can learn from verses 8-9?

Day 74, 2 Nephi 33

We have spent a considerable amount of time with the prophet Nephi. Today we will bid him—and he will bid us—farewell. These will not be the only goodbyes though. For some, the last time they will see Heavenly Father and Jesus Christ will be at the judgment bar. What does Nephi teach us in this chapter about how to stay in their presence?

What do verses 1-2 teach us about receiving or rejecting spiritual lessons from the Holy Ghost?

In verses 3-7, look for what hopes Nephi had for his record, the Book of Mormon. Which of Nephi's hopes and prayers do you believe have been realized in your own life?

Day 75, Jacob 1

How do Nephi's instructions to Jacob about what to write in the small plates in verses 1-4, also make great instructions for how to study the small plates?

Anxiety is not traditionally seen as a good thing, yet Jacob adds it as an almost prerequisite, along with faith, to receive revelation (:5-6). What role might anxiety play in the revelatory process?

Verses 15-16 lay out the problems that Jacob will address in the next chapter.

Do you find verse 19 to be motivational, informational, or terrifying? What connection exists between us magnifying our callings so that Christ can then magnify His own calling? Consider the garment and the blood mentioned at the end of the verse.

Day 76, Jacob 2:1-21

What are some of the lessons and principles that Jacob teaches us about leadership in verses 1-11?

Jacob teaches that the purpose of most teaching is to heal the wounded soul (:9). Will you watch for those moments this week as you study the word of God?

In verses 12-21, Jacob addresses the first of two issues. What is the problem of seeking riches and position, and what solutions does Jacob offer?

Day 77, Jacob 2:22-35

The second problem that Jacob was dealing with was polygamy. As you read today's section, look for all of the reasons for and against polygamy or plural marriage. Which of these reasons for or against are doctrinal?

One of these reasons is found in verse 30. What is the difference between raising up seed/children versus raising up seed/children unto the Lord?

There are several times in verses 31-35 that the tears and pains of God's women and daughters are noticed and matched by him. Do you think any of those tears or sorrows were ignored when God, for a brief time, commanded plural marriage at the beginning of the restoration?

For more information on this subject go to the "Gospel Topics" page on lds.org and look up "Plural Marriage in the Church of Jesus Christ of Latter-day Saints." Or Google "plural marriage lds gospel topics" and then select a link that leads you to lds.org. You can also go to the "Church History" icon on the Gospel Library home page, then click on "Gospel Topics…." You can then read the three essays that the Church has produced regarding this topic.

Day 78, Jacob 3

What promises and counsel are given to those who are "pure in heart" and to those who are not?

By the end of the Book of Mormon, it is the Nephites that are destroyed and not the Lamanites. What do verses 5-7 teach us about the why this is? What does that teach you about the importance of family relationships between parents and children and between husband and wife?

At this time what do the Nephites misunderstand about race and filthiness (:3-4, 8-12)?

Day 79, Jacob 4

What can we learn about writing on the metal plates from Jacob's sayings in verses 1-3?

The purpose of everything that Jacob and Nephi wrote was to point their family and others toward Christ and a belief in Him. On a paper, write down the phrase "Christ is the mark." Then, as you read verses 4-13, list all the things mentioned in those verses that help point us to Christ, arranging them around the phrase with arrows pointing in toward the phrase.

In addition to verses 4-13 pointing us toward Christ, there are several really impressive teachings in those verses. Study each of the following sections and try to record at least one gem that they teach you (:4-5, 6-7, 8-9, 10, and 11-13).

Today we will also learn about others who missed Christ and stumbled. On your paper write, "Christ is the mark," but this time you will list things around the phrase from verses 14-15 that caused people to miss Christ, with arrows pointing away from Christ to those things listed. What other things might you add that have the potential to lead you away from Christ?

Day 80, Jacob 5:1-18

Jacob begins to tell the allegory of the olive tree that Zenos, an ancient prophet, taught. It is symbolic of the history of the Jews and Gentiles. As of yet, there is no external evidence outside of the Book of Mormon that Zenos lived and was a prophet.

As you read today's section, look for examples of the master of the vineyard's love and devotion.

"It grieveth me that I should lose this tree" (:7, 11). These words are spoken by the master of the vineyard, who represents the Lord. What words could you substitute in place of the word "tree" that would more accurately express what he is truly concerned about?

Which historic events do you think match up with the allegory we have read?

Day 81, Jacob 5:19-34

The master of the vineyard's success depends upon how well he can help his tree produce good fruit. Do you think this is an accurate analogy when speaking about God?

Notice what kind of ground these two trees, which produced good fruit, were planted in (:21-23). The production of good fruit was possible because the master of the vineyard provided nourishment. Who do you know that, despite poor circumstances, responded to the nourishment of the Lord and produced a life of goodness?

Have you figured out which tree represents the Jews and the Gentiles and which one represents the Nephites and Lamanites?

In yesterday and today's sections, the words "nourish" and "nourished" are used a lot. What principles can we learn about development from pondering upon those words? Notice that he "nourished" the tree in verse 22 for a "long time."

Day 82, Jacob 5:35-48

On the third visit to the vineyard, the master and servant found all of the trees had become corrupt, representing a state of apostasy.

What can verses 35, 41, and 47 help us understand about how God feels and reacts when his children choose wickedness over righteousness?

We get the words "overcome" and "overrun" several times in today's verses. What does verse 48 say about why this overcoming happened and what we can do to prevent it from happening to us?

Day 83, Jacob 5:49-69

Consider all that the master has done to this point for his vineyard, and then consider all that he will do for it (49). He is far more committed to the salvation of these trees than the trees are. What would happen if we put forth a little more effort to match his, both for ourselves and others?

What do verses 50-51 teach us about the relationship between the Lord and His prophets?

41

Even before the church was restored, before there were any members, the Book of Mormon spoke of the servants who would be called (:61). In what ways have you been allowed to help fulfill this prophecy by laboring alongside the Lord in His vineyard?

The branches represent different groups of people, and the fruit their works. What do you think the roots, that are so frequently mentioned in today's section could represent?

Day 84, Jacob 5:70-77

In verses 70-75, look for what is included in being a servant of the master. When have you felt the master of the vineyard laboring next to you in this great work (:72)?

In Jacob 4:16-18, we were told the reason why the allegory of the olive tree was given. Now that you have studied it, how would you answer the question in Jacob 4:17?

Day 85, Jacob 6

What evidence can you find in this chapter that the following statement is true? "When it comes to salvation and exaltation, God says yes until we say no."

According to verses 5-8, what must a person harden, reject, deny, quench, and mock in order not to accept salvation offered through Christ?

Why do you think that verse 12 is a good logical conclusion to verses 9-11?

Day 86, Jacob 7:1-23

There have always been people who seek to destroy the faith and beliefs of others. Sherem, was such a man. What were the attitudes, attributes, and arguments that made Sherem so good at destroying the faith of others?

Sherem wanted to shake the faith of Jacob, but Jacob had a list of experiences that made it so he could not be shaken (:5). Mentally list the spiritual experiences that you have had that would make up your own list to remind you when the would-be faith-shakers come along?

What important lesson can verses 10-11 teach us about the scriptures?

Why do you think the Lord doesn't show such signs when faith-shakers show up in your life? What signs does the Lord show instead?

Notice what the people do in verse 23 after they have had an experience with a person who tried to shake their faith. Why do you think this was an important choice for the people to make?

Day 87, Jacob 7:24-Enos 1:18

Some people have been critical of the word "adieu" in Jacob's final farewell by asking: how could a French word make its way into a book written in Reformed Egyptian by Hebrew authors? Nephi already explained that the Lord speaks unto us after the manner of our own language (2 Nephi 31:3). We also learn a little bit about the translation process from the instruction given to Oliver Cowdery during his attempt (D&C 8-9). Thus, the ideas of ancient prophets are translated into words that are familiar to Joseph Smith by the power of the Holy Ghost. The word "adieu" was a common farewell in the time of Joseph Smith.

With Enos' call to be the record keeper/prophet came the ensuing unworthiness that we have all felt, to some degree, following a calling from the Lord. We love these verses because of their incredibly honest and concise prayers. Search for an idea, phrase, or word in each of the following sections that inspires you. Verses 1-8 are about Enos' prayer for himself. Verses 9-10 is his prayer for the Nephites. Verses 11-14 is his prayer for the Lamanites. And verses 15-18 is his prayer for the records or scriptures.

What things will you diligently pray over and for today?

Day 88, Enos 1:19-27

Look at all the different ways that the Lamanites are described in verse 20. Even with their fixed hatred toward the Nephites, the Nephites sought diligently to restore them. What principle are we to learn from that? How can we use that principle with family members, former friends, neighbors, and enemies who seem to have a fixed hatred toward us?

What does verse 23 teach you about the purpose of hellfire and brimstone preaching?

A huge chunk of the Plan of Salvation is contained in verse 27. Read each line and consider which significant doctrine about the plan is being covered.

Day 89, Jarom

As you read today's section, look for what kept the Nephites from being destroyed by the Lamanites. Which of those things offer you current protection?

When we speak of the Plan of Salvation, we often think of circles and arrows, yet Jarom mentioned that Nephi, Jacob, and Enos had already revealed the Plan of Salvation (:2). They didn't speak about the premortal life or the three degrees of glory. What did they reveal then about the Plan of Salvation?

Verse 4 mentions that there are many who receive revelations if they are "not stiffnecked and have faith". In what ways have you received revelation this week?

Read verse 11 then finish this sentence: "The purpose of the Law of Moses was . . ."

When was the last time you felt your heart pricked as you studied the scriptures or the words of prophets? Do you think all pricks are to stir us to repentance? What other types of pricks may there be?

Day 90, Omni 1:1-11

Today we will meet four more authors of the Book of Mormon. Which one do you think best represents how well you keep your journal and record sacred experiences?

When reading verse 2, people have tried to decide if Omni is wicked or humble. What do you think, and what are the lessons we are to learn from him if he is humble or wicked?

What examples can you think of when God's word was verified (:6)?

Why is the idea of sufficiency mentioned in verse 11 dangerous (see 2 Nephi 28:30)?

Day 91, Omni 1:12-30

Today's section contains the meeting and interaction of several different groups. See what you can learn about each group. King Mosiah 1 and his people are found in verses 12-13. Zarahemla, the people of Zarahemla, and the land of Zarahemla are in verses 14-19. Coriantumr, the last of the Jaredites, is in verses 20-22. King Benjamin is in verses 23-25. And, Zeniff and his people, who wanted to return to the Land of Nephi, are verses 27-30.

What do verses 12-13 teach us about how to receive protection and direction?

According to verse 17, what happens to belief when scriptures are no longer available or read?

What does Amaleki invite and promise us in verses 25-26?

Day 92, The Words of Mormon

From the end of Omni to The Words of Mormon, we skip from 130 B.C. to 385 A.D. The Words of Mormon were added to bridge the gap between the large and small plates of Nephi. The small plates were included at the end of the golden plates along with The Words of Mormon and the title page. The small plates of Nephi (1 Nephi - Omni) cover the same time period as the 116 pages that were lost by Martin Harris. Joseph Smith didn't know of this back-up plan until after the incident (D&C 10). As you read Words of Mormon 1:1-11, look for why Mormon included the small plates. This incident increased the resolve of Joseph Smith. How will it increase your resolve to do what God asks?

The books of 1 Nephi through Omni were added because of a "whisper" (:7). What unknown benefits might come to you, your family, and others today, because you will follow the whispers from the Spirit today?

Look for how King Benjamin, a new king, must deal with both external and internal conflicts in verses 12-18. King Benjamin was a holy man and, with the help of other holy men, did great things. Our world, our towns, and our families are all in need of holy men and women, and King Benjamin is going to teach us how to become such in the next few chapters.

Day 93, Mosiah 1:1-14

As you read verses 1-8, look for reasons why Mosiah taught his children, and what he decided to teach them.

According to verses 3-7, what happens to people who lose or disregard the scriptures? What will you do to become like King Benjamin and endear yourself, your family, and others to the scriptures?

With each covenant we make there are names that accompany it. It is no different with King Benjamin giving his people a name. They have kept their covenants thus far and are now ready for their next covenant (:9-14). Consider King Benjamin's proclamation to his people. It is a proclamation as well as an invitation to you. What is the next covenant that you need to make?

Day 94, Mosiah 1:15-2:8

What did King Benjamin charge Mosiah to take care of in Mosiah 1:15-16? What charges have been assigned to you?

What can we learn about how to prepare for temple worship, General Conference, or any other meeting from King Benjamin and his people in Mosiah 2:1-8? What will you do to be ready for your next meeting?

Day 95, Mosiah 2:9-27

What would happen if we approached every talk or lesson the way verses 9-11 suggest?

What does King Benjamin teach us and his people about what it means to be a leader in verses 12-27?

Verse 21 calls us unprofitable servants if we do all we can. According to verses 23-26 why is this the case?

Day 96, Mosiah 2:28-41

Often in General Conference we see some of the prophets, looking weak and shaky in body, deliver their addresses despite physical ailments, and so it was with King Benjamin (:28-30). This shakiness in body is not weakness in spirit, but instead a testimony of the commitment and devotion they feel toward their people and their responsibility. May we adore those who wear out their bodies in the service of their fellow beings and Master.

In verses 31-41, what does King Benjamin teach about the states of the righteous and the wicked and how they arrived at those states? Have you been able discern the difference between when you are drinking damnation and exhalation through your daily choices?

Verse 41 proclaims that those who keep the commandments are "blessed in all things, both temporal and spiritual." Often, I feel that the temporal part of that promise is downplayed, but if we were to look at the right parts of our lives, with eyes to see, we would discover that this promise is true. If you pray to become more aware of those temporal blessings, revelation will show there are several subtle and significant temporal blessings being showered down upon you for obedience to the commandments. When this happens, I invite you to become more thankful for these specific blessings in your prayers.

Day 97, Mosiah 3:1-19

What sources do you use when giving a talk? Look for the sources that King Benjamin used in his own talk in verses 1-4.

Verses 5-10 contain a prophecy about the life and ministry of Jesus Christ. As you read, look for words or phrases that help you better appreciate the mission of Jesus Christ.

Verses 11-19 contain information about who are saved through the Atonement and how they are saved. It would be worth your time to write down each group that is mentioned. Then, carefully consider how the salvation of each group is an incredible demonstration of the love and mercy of the Father and the Son.

Verse 19 is worth several slow reads, a lot of pondering, and maybe even a little writing to help clarify your thoughts.

Day 98, Mosiah 3:19-4:3

That's right, Mosiah 3:19 made the reading list again. Yesterday, did you use faith in the Atonement and the Holy Ghost to put off the natural man, or did you just try to change by yourself? This verse is deserving of several more reads, of more pondering, and even a few more words put to paper.

The first part of Mosiah 3 was about who is saved through the Atonement and how they are saved. Verses 20-27 are about who is damned through the Atonement and how. People rarely drink things that they didn't intend to drink. Likewise the drinking of damnation will not be an accident.

What are some things you do each day to get clean? In Mosiah 4:1-3 the people of King Benjamin become clean. As you read those verses, look for what they did to become clean and what cleansed them. From what you learned, how can you know if you are spiritually clean?

Day 99, Mosiah 4:4-15

Which do you think is harder: getting little kids clean or keeping them clean? What do you think Heavenly Father and Jesus Christ would say?

Yesterday we learned about how to become clean. In verses 4-13 we will learn how to remain clean.

Why is it important for us to believe each of the things mentioned in verses 9-10?

If the only parenting training someone received was through verses 14-15, how well do you think they would do?

Day 100, Mosiah 4:16-30

One of the fundamental purposes of being a Christian is to take care of the poor. Today's section contains one of the greatest discourses on that subject. What do you think are the major things that we should learn about our treatment of the poor from verses 16-26?

Why is verse 27 good counsel, not just for helping the poor but for everything?

How many different ways to sin can you think of in the next 30 seconds? Now we all can understand the words of verse 29 and the warning and advice of verse 30 to "watch," "observe," and "continue."

Which of the following do you most need today: to watch thoughts, words, and deeds; observe commandments; or continue in faith?

Day 101, Mosiah 5

This is an incredible chapter on what motivates us to make sacred covenants, what those covenants mean, and why we must remember them. Some keywords to watch for today that will help you see these themes are: spirit, change, covenant, called, name, and remember. When you are done with your study, answer the following question: What important thing did you learn about covenants?

How did the Holy Ghost help people become ready to make sacred covenants in verses 1-3?

When we accept the gospel and make sacred covenants, we also become the sons and daughters of Jesus Christ because He is the Father of the covenant (:7-8, D&C 25:1).

John 17:3 states that in order to have eternal life, we must know Heavenly Father and Jesus Christ. Mosiah 5:13 offers a remarkable insight into how we can come to know them better. How will you apply that verse today?

Day 102, Mosiah 6:1-7:6

What does King Benjamin do in 6:1-3 to help his people honor their covenants after they have made them?

The rule and reign of King Mosiah is described in 6:4-7. Do you think the same things said about his leadership could be said of your personal leadership both in and outside of your home?

It has been 79 years, and no contact, since the people of Zeniff went up to inhabit the land of Nephi (Omni 1:27-30). What are some of the lessons about rescuing others that we can learn from the story in 7:1-6?

Day 103, Mosiah 7:7-33

Yesterday, we left Ammon in the bonds of captivity. Today, we will be caught up to date on the people of Zeniff and all that has happened since they left the people of King Benjamin to return to the Land of Nephi, which was being occupied by the Lamanites. If you can keep all of that straight you deserve a treat.

Watch for what led to their captivity and what the Lord is already doing to prepare for their deliverance. Do you think today will be a day that you will help deliver others or that you will need delivering? Either way, that is what the Lord does.

Limhi gives a wonderful summary of Abinadi's life and teachings of Christ in verses 26-28. What did you like about this summary, and what would you add to complete it?

Day 104, Mosiah 8

In verses 1-12, Ammon and King Limhi continue to catch each other up on what has happened. Look for which teachings each thought was most important. How would you summarize what has happened in The Church of Jesus Christ of Latter-day Saints in the last 80 years?

In verses 13-18, Ammon explains the purpose and blessings of having a seer. This is one of the best places in all scripture to learn about the definition of a seer. So, carefully read and ponder what you will learn about seers.

How have seers been a "great benefit" to you in your life (:18)?

What comparisons can you make between the interpreters—or Urim and Thummim—and cell phones or electronic devices by studying verse 13?

Day 105, Mosiah 9

The storyline of Ammon and King Limhi is interrupted as we travel back 79 years to the beginning of Zeniff's journeys. Zeniff is Limhi's grandfather.

Zeniff describes his desire to retain the land of Nephi as over-zealousness (:3). We have all had times when our passion to achieve something that we want causes us to make mistakes in judgment. Is there anything in your life that the spirit might be warning you that you are over-zealous in?

In what way can the enabling power of the Atonement be seen in verses 14-18? How will use the enabling power of the Atonement today in your life? (See also "grace" in the Bible Dictionary).

Day 106, Mosiah 10

What did Limhi and his people do to obtain peace and protection for 22 years in verses 1-10?

King Limhi's people received strength as they relied on the Lord. The Lamanites' strength was in their own arm (:10-11, 19). In your experience, what is the difference between doing something in the strength of the Lord versus relying on your own strength?

According to verses 12-18, on what false traditions and premises did the Lamanites base their eternal hatred for the Nephites? What are some of the false traditions and premises that lead to misunderstanding and disagreement within the Church today? Because of our understanding about God and the Plan of Salvation, our beliefs may often start in very different places than the beliefs of others.

Day 107, Mosiah 11:1-15

As you read, look for the desires of the new king and what influence it had upon his people.

What difference do you notice between King Noah and King Benjamin? What difference does it make to your family when you lead with the thoughts and desires of King Benjamin rather than the thoughts and desires of King Noah?

Why do you think a group of people, who in the last chapter trusted in the Lord, would support a leader who trusted in everything but the Lord?

Day 108, Mosiah 11:16-29

Yesterday, we read about the many poor choices of King Noah, a trend he will continue today. What new leadership blunders do you see King Noah do in verses 16-19?

In verses 20-25, we are introduced to Abinadi. Watch for how bold and directly he speaks for the Lord with words and phrases like: "except," "I will," and "it shall." Does the Lord have to use such direct language with you or can he get you to respond to gentle nudges?

Upon hearing about what Abinadi had said, King Noah responded the way that many people do, by playing the "you shouldn't judge" card (:27). How does this misunderstood doctrine about judgment prevent the guilty party from repenting?

In verse 29, we learn that the people were blinded. In what ways were they blinded in how they viewed both Abinadi and King Noah? Who was their real friend? What modern day examples have you seen that demonstrate this same type of blindness?

Day 109, Mosiah 12:1-16

Look for all of the different prophecies that Abinadi makes in verses 1-12.

How do the people of King Noah explain away the prophet Abinadi and his words in verses 12-15? Which of those reasons do people also use today to excuse themselves from having to accept the prophets and their words?

In verse 16, the people leave Abinadi with King Noah to "do with him as seemeth thee good." Each of us also makes a choice about what we will do with the prophets.

Day 110, Mosiah 12:17-13:4

In Mosiah 13:17-24, we read about the priests of King Noah who question Abinadi. Their question about the Isaiah passage makes more sense when you realize they are calling Abinadi a bad prophet because he didn't publish peace, but rather declared prophecies of destruction.

In Mosiah 13:25-37, look for the corrections that Abinadi now gives to the wishy-washy watchmen who are King Noah's priests. What are the different ways that they failed in their trusted roles as leaders and teachers?

What do you love about Mosiah 13:1-4?

In what ways has Abinadi set an example for what a true leader and teacher should be?

Day 111, Mosiah 13:5-35

In verses 11-26, Abinadi teaches the commandments to King Noah and his priests. How do you think a person gets the commandments written in their hearts (:11)? Out of all of the commandments, why do you think the Sabbath day gets the most verses and emphasis (:16-19)? What do verses 25-26 teach you about the relationship between keeping the Ten Commandments and feeling worthy and clean before God and his prophets?

Abinadi delivers one of the greatest discourses on the Law of Moses and its connection with Christ and the Atonement in verses 27-35. When did you have the change of heart so that God didn't have to give you strict commandments, promptings, and assignments to get you to remember and choose good?

Day 112, Mosiah 14:1-15:9

In chapter 14, Abinadi quotes Isaiah 53, with each verse containing incredible prophecies about the Savior, His ministry, and Atonement. Does verse 2 change the way that you view the Savior? In verses 3-6, notice what He does for us and what we do to Him. How could it have pleased Heavenly Father to bruise his Son (:10)? What do you think it means when it says Jesus will "see his seed..." "...when he makes an offering for sin" (:10)?

With deep significance in every phrase, which idea about the Savior in Mosiah 14 did the Holy Ghost help you feel the importance of or understand more clearly?

Day 113, Mosiah 15:10-31

Yesterday, we pondered upon the possibility of Christ seeing his seed while He suffered for their sins. Today, in verses 10-18, we learn from Abinadi more about who His seed is. Who is His seed and who has beautiful feet?

In verses 19-21, look for what would happen without Christ and what will happen because of Christ?

What do we learn about who does and who does not get to participate in the first resurrection according to verses 22-27?

Verses 28-31 speak about a time that "shall come." What evidence is there that this time has, is, or is still to come?

Day 114, Mosiah 16

From what you read today, look for how many different ways you can complete the following phrases:

Because of Christ . . .
Because of Satan . . .
Because there is a Christ I will . . .
Because there is a Satan I will . . .

Day 115, Mosiah 17

When a prophet of God is accused and diminished, how does Alma show his new kindled devotion (:1-4)? When have you had the opportunity to demonstrate your devotion to prophets? Without Alma writing the words of Abinadi, we would not have them. What changes have come into the lives of others lately because of a reaction you have had with the words of prophets?

In verses 8-10, Abinadi refuses to "recall" his words or his testimony, and instead lets them "stand." There are a few who have recalled their testimonies and previous feelings about the restored gospel. When the challenge comes to "recall" your words and testimony, I invite you to let your words and witness "stand" as Abinadi did.

King Noah let "fear" and "anger" direct his choices (:11-12). Which one of these feelings confused you into doing something you regretted this week? What is the difference between how you feel when you allow faith, courage, love, understanding, patience, and other Christlike attitudes to counsel us in our actions?

Day 116, Mosiah 18:1-16

The land of Mormon was known for two things: wild beasts and a fountain of pure water (:4-5). This is also an accurate description for each member of the church. Sometimes we are a little more beast than pure water, and at other times we let the pure fountain wash over the animal in us. Which will dominate your choices and thoughts today?

Verses 8-10 give us one of the best places in all scripture to study about the covenants that we make when we are baptized. As you study these verses, it may be helpful to list, number, or mark the promises that we make and also the promises that God makes. Do you think these promises are of equal value? In which of these promises have you found particular pleasure? As you have come to better understand the baptismal covenant, how has it impacted your life and the lives of others for good?

If you were attending the baptismal service found in verses 12-16, what things might you have thought were peculiar or different about the baptism? What do you think might be some reasons for these differences? With a little Google searching, you might also find an explanation from President Joseph Fielding Smith.

Day 117, Mosiah 18:17-35

Alma and his little band of church members are incredible. Look for everything we can learn about what it means to be a member of Christ's church in verses 17-29. Which of those teachings have brought tremendous blessings and joy into your life?

In verse 30, we learn that all of these things happened in and around the land and waters of Mormon. Later, Mormon will tell us that he was named Mormon because of these events and this place (3 Nephi 5:12). The Book of Mormon teaches us how to make, and then keep, sacred covenants. These lands and waters of Mormon are beautiful to those who came to know their Redeemer there. Likewise, I have a fondness for an old rolltop desk where, as a teenager, I studied the scriptures and gained a testimony. Where or what is your land and water of Mormon, where you gained your love and knowledge of your Redeemer?

Day 118, Mosiah 19

For several chapters, the people of King Noah have been blind to his faults, but not today. Today, they come to know what he really is as he abandons women and children in an attempt to save his own life (:11). There are King Noahs in our own lives who quietly ask us to leave spouses, children, and home for personal comfort, pleasure, and prestige. We are blind if we believe these lies, and we will end up as bitter and angry at our Noahs as his people were with him. They couldn't even bring themselves to shoulder the blame; they had to take it out on him (:20). What will you do to make sure you don't suffer from King Noah blindness and sacrifice that which is most important because of lies and false promises? Look for all of the consequences throughout this chapter that King Noah and the people listening to him brought upon themselves. What form does King Noah take in your life?

Day 119, Mosiah 20

In verses 1-5, we will see that the wicked priests of King Noah continue making terrible choices that affect the lives of others. Look for the different reasons given in verse 3 about why this group would not return and repent. Those reasons match the thoughts and feelings of many today who likewise will not return or repent. Why do you think it is important for us to daily return to God and repent? What are some of the dangers of delaying repentance?

The Lamanites waged a war with the people of Limhi because of a misunderstanding (:6-7, 15). How often do we go to war with others in our hearts, minds, and homes because of misunderstandings?

In verses 16-26, look for the efforts that King Limhi goes through to end misunderstanding and restore peace. Use the following words or phrases to help you identify some of these principles and truths: "searched" (:16-17), "pacified/pacify" (:19-22, 26), and "without arms" (:24-26).

Day 120, Mosiah 21:1-21

There are consequences when we chose to disobey the commandments of God. Abinadi had warned the people of this back in Mosiah 12. Look for how his words and warning are now being fulfilled in verses 1-4. Since this type of slavery is uncommon in our day, what would you say are some modern day examples of consequences that people suffer for not listening to the prophets warnings?

In verse 5 we are told that the people could not have delivered themselves. Their attempts are recorded in verses 6-12. Are there things in your life that you are trying to accomplish without the assistance of the Lord? Are there goals that you have written and declared, but have not yet prayed and pleaded for? How many times do you have to try things on your own until you turn to the Lord for help and direction?

What changes occurred in the lives of King Limhi and his people when they turned to heaven for help (:13-16)? Do you think it is difficult for people to see how the Lord "eases their burdens" (:15) or how they "prosper by degrees" (:16)? Will you look for the ease and degrees in your life today?

Day 121, Mosiah 21:22-36

Look for the difference that Ammon and his little group were able to make in the life of King Limhi and his people.

What things can verse 33 teach us about priesthood authority?

King Limhi and his people were "desirous to become like" Alma and his people (:34). What do you desire to become?

I really like that "all the study of Ammon and his people, and King Limhi and his people was to deliver themselves" (:34). What things are you putting forth effort to study in addition to the scriptures?

Day 122, Mosiah 22

What examples of effective listening and strong councils do you see in verses 1-9? In what ways is Gideon a good example of what a member of a council should be? How has listening to the suggestions of others in councils helped provide deliverance for people?

There are subtle miracles in this story, but the Lord had them play a bigger role in "delivering themselves" than others, as we will see (:1-2). Why do you think it is important that, at times, we also have to work at delivering ourselves without the mighty miracles?

Day 123, Mosiah 23:1-15

The Lord provided both warning and strength to Alma and his people (:1-2). What warnings and strengths has heaven provided you in the last week?

The people wanted Alma to be their King, but he declined. In verses 6-14, look for the different principles Alma gave in defense of his refusal.

Repentance is real and wonderful, but there is a price that we must pay according to verses 9-11.

Nearly every relationship we have will benefit from the teaching found in verse 15; love more, fight less. The whole day after writing the previous sentence, I have continued to think about its simple message. I have loved more and fought less. It was a good day. What difference will this teaching of Christ make in your life today?

Day 124, Mosiah 23:16-39

What principles can we learn from verses 21-24? What evidence has there been in your life that God does show forth his mighty power to deliver people?

Why is it important that Alma's people hushed their fears (:27-28)? What do you think Alma knew about fear and its effects on people?

Sometimes our poor choices in the past continue to make our present, and even our future, more difficult. Alma and his people have changed their lives in an incredible fashion, but their association with Amulon and his wicked priests in the past have now returned to haunt them (:30-39). In the coming chapter, watch for how the Lord teaches the subtle lesson that we can each be completely delivered from our past choices even if they still haunt us for a time.

Day 125, Mosiah 24:1-15

Amulon and his wicked priests were appointed to be teachers to the Lamanites. Look for what they taught and what they did not teach in verses 1-7. Why is it important to have a balance in the things that we teach and learn?

As you read verses 10-12, look for what Amulon understood about prayer and what he did not. What assurances have you had in your life that God is aware of and responsive to silent prayers of the heart?

What do verses 13-15 say about how the Atonement of Christ is used to provide deliverance to us in times of affliction? In what ways can a slow but strengthening delivery show how loving our Lord is?

Day 126, Mosiah 24:16-25:14

As you read Mosiah 24:16-25, look for the differences between the deliverance of Alma and his people compared to King Limhi and his people. Why do you think God was more obvious in one than the other? Why is Mosiah 24:22-23 an important part of the story?

In Mosiah 25:1-11, look for the different feelings and emotions that the Nephites and the people of Zarahemla demonstrate when they hear the accounts of deliverance. How have you benefited from the faith, testimony, and stories of others in the last few months?

How would you complete the following sentence after reading Mosiah 25:12)? "Pedigree determines much, but . . ."

Day 127, Mosiah 25:15-26:13

With the arrival of Alma and his people, we will see the church begin to flourish. In Mosiah 25:15-24, notice how the structure of the church had to change to accommodate the new growth. How did this new structure bless the lives of the church members?

The Church of God is always one generation away from apostasy. In Mosiah 26:1-13, look for why this new generation struggled to believe. What effect did their unbelief have on themselves, others, and the church?

What would you have done, and what can you do to try to prevent unbelief in the rising generation?

Day 128, Mosiah 26:13-39

Alma was confused and troubled about how to deal with members who were sinning and not repenting. How do Alma's actions in verses 13-14 set an example for what we should do when we find ourselves troubled about what to do?

Verses 14-32 contain the Lord's answer to Alma regarding those members who refuse to repent. What counsel did the Lord give? How might this counsel be useful in helping those who are struggling with unbelief? Look for how involved the Lord is with His church, covenants, and members by noticing the words: "my," "I," and "mine."

In the midst of his great concern for others, the Lord promised Alma eternal life, or made his calling and election sure (:20). That is fantastic for him, and also very useful to us. If you thought back and recalled everything that we learned about Alma since we met him, and made a list of what he did, you would have the instructions for how to also receive eternal life.

Day 129, Mosiah 27:1-17

After reading verses 1-7, pick one of the following words and use it in a sentence about what you learned: persecution, proclamation, peace, prosper.

In the last chapter, we saw that some members of the church were numbered among the unbelievers and their names were blotted out (Mosiah 26:34-36). In Mosiah 27:8-10, look for who was included in this group and what impact they were having on others. What lessons do you think we can learn from this?

Today, we have people who also seek the destruction of the church. What did the angel say in verse 13 about what can and cannot hurt the church? What does that mean we can do to help protect the church?

What can we learn about the power of prayer from verses 14-16? How long and sincerely do you think they had been praying? Will you please continue to pray for the "Alma the Youngers" in your life? Why is it important to know that when we can't get through to a family member, God will send an angel to them at some point, in whatever form that may be?

Day 130, Mosiah 27:18-37

How do verses 18-23 show the goodness and power of God?

How does Alma describe what happened to him in verses 24-31? Which word or phrase of Alma's description do you find most captivating? What words would you use to describe the change that Christ caused to happen to you?

What evidence is there in verses 32-37 that the change that Alma and the sons of Mosiah experienced is permanent and their repentance real? What evidence is there in your own life that you, like Alma, have experienced a mighty change, even if it didn't come as fast as his?

Day 131, Mosiah 28

Sometimes people desire to serve missions because of social pressures. Look for all of the reasons that the sons of Mosiah wanted to serve in verses 1-5. Which of those desires match your own reasons for wanting to share the gospel?

Verse 4 proclaims that these sons of Mosiah and Alma were the "vilest of sinners." One of my favorite connections in the Book of Mormon is to link verse 4 to Alma 48:17-18 and consider how these same men are described there. What do these verses teach about the power of the Atonement? When have you experienced or witnessed this power?

Look for how the faith of their father in verses 6-9 would bless the lives of the sons of Mosiah for chapters to come.

Verses 10-20 speak of the translation of the Jaredite records by means of the Urim and Thummim/interpreters and the transference of these things from Mosiah to Alma the Younger. The Urim and Thummim were among the tools that the Lord allowed Joseph Smith to use while translating the Book of Mormon. For more information, check out the "Book of Mormon Translation" section of the "Gospel Topic Essays" under the "Church History" icon on the Gospel Library app. Why do you think the Lord is willing to provide physical aids, like the staff of Moses, Liahona, and seer stones, to increase the faith and ability of his prophets? What are some of the tools the Lord has provided to do this in our day?

Day 131, Mosiah 29:1-15

The Nephites have just had three righteous kings in a row with King Mosiah I, King Benjamin, and then King Mosiah II. In the midst of this dynasty of holy kings, look for the reasons King Mosiah II gives for why the people shouldn't have a king in verses 1-15. Which reasons do you agree with?

What principles of leadership does King Mosiah II also teach us in these same verses?

In what ways could leadership or political power cause the destruction of someone (:10)?

Day 132, Mosiah 29:16-32

Today, King Mosiah continues his warnings about the impact a wicked king can have in verses 16-23. What kinds of similar things can be said about a wicked father, mother, friend, leader, or teacher?

What can we learn about the relationship between laws and leaders?

After two days of talking about the powerful influence of kings, we will now be introduced to another power player, "the voice of the people." As you search verses 24-32, what is the difference between having a king and the power of the people, with its accompanying accountability? What does the "voice of the people" sound like in your family, neighborhood, community, and country?

Day 133, Mosiah 29:33-47

In verses 33-37, King Mosiah explains the hardships of being a king. He must expand their vision before they will want to take on the responsibility of selecting judges. When has a great leader expanded your vision?

In verse 38, the people "relinquished their desires for a king." Growth, development, and change will always require that we relinquish something. What thoughts, feelings, attitudes, desires, words, or actions has the Holy Ghost been nudging you to relinquish lately?

Verses 41-47 contain the account of the appointment of the first chief judge.

Day 134, Alma 1:1-14

Be ready to write or share with someone your ideas about the following themes in today's section:

Popularity
Pride
Persecution
Priestcraft
Punishment

Day 135, Alma 1:15-33

Today we will continue to examine themes:

Punishment
Persecution
Pride
Preaching
Peace and prosperity
Poverty

When you are finished reading, what additional insights could you have added to your list from yesterday?

In what ways are verses 24-25 important then, now, and in the future?

Why do you think it is necessary for the teacher and the learner to believe that they really are equals (:26)? What difference can this verse make in your Sunday school class?

Day 136, Alma 2:1-18

As you read today's section, consider what would or could have happened if the voice of the people would have remained politically silent. Why do you think it is important for members of the church to be politically aware and involved, even though the church avoids involvement in many political issues?

There are always things and people that are seeking to draw us to or away from things (:2-3). What things are you being drawn toward and what things are you being drawn away from today?

In verses 12-18 we learn that both the Nephites and the Amlicites prepared for battle and appointed leaders. What made the difference for the Nephites so that they started to prevail?

Day 137, Alma 2:19-38

As you read verses 19-26, look for all of the different things Alma does to try to protect his people and their families. What type of tactical protections are you initiating in your home and for your family?

One of the most common themes in the Book of Mormon is found when people are placed in a position where the odds are against them. There are key principles about the Atonement and prayer that we are continually being taught in those situations. Look for these principles as you read verses 27-31.

Today, you and your family will not face off against Amlicites or Lamanites, but you will be placed in a situation where the odds are against you. How will you use the principles you have learned to win the day?

Day 138, Alma 3:1-19

After reading today's section, how would you explain the difference between a "mark" and a "curse?"

Why is it significant that the Amlicites "marked themselves" (:4)?

According to verses 7-8, what was one purpose for the Lord placing a mark upon people? Why is it important to know that the Lord was not trying to separate the Nephites from skin color, but false traditions and teachings, when a mark was placed upon the Lamanites?

Just as there were marks for what makes a Lamanite, so there are also marks for what made a Nephite (:11). What marks are you putting on your life to show what you believe?

Day 139, Alma 3:20-4:4

How do you think Alma felt about not being able to go to battle with those that he sent (3:20-24)? What is the difference between being able and being willing? What lessons do you think this experience taught Alma about himself and others?

In what ways do the words "reap," "listed/listeth," or "wages" help us understand the principle being taught in Alma 3:26-27? How will this principle help us in the choices that we will have to make today?

As you read Alma 4:1-4, consider whether the battles and death impacted the people and the church in the way you thought they would.

Day 140, Alma 4:5-20

What do verses 5-12 teach us about the development of pride and the results of pride? What possibilities do you have for pride in your own life? What do you think you can do to slow the growth of pride in yourself?

While pride was raging in many church members, there was also a group of members who were retaining a remission of their sins and being filled with great joy. Look for how they did it in verses 13-14. What can you do to retain a remission of your sins and be filled with joy?

What truths about politics and religion can we learn from the actions of Alma in verses 15-20?

When was a time in your life that you were moved because of the power of a pure testimony (:19)?

Day 141, Alma 5:1-25

Today's section has nearly enough of its own questions for us to answer, but here are just a few more.

How would you finish the following phrase: "A change of heart is like. . ."

For the questions in verses 15-16, and 19, answer each through one of the following: always, frequently, usually, sometimes, not often, or not at all.

Why do you think Alma uses words like "received" and "engraven" Christ's image on our countenance rather than print or place?

If you were Alma, what questions would you add for a modern audience?

Day 142, Alma 5:26-42

Alma still has some more questions for you to answer.

When was the last time you accepted the invitation of the Lord offered in verse 32?

In what ways is it good to frequently repent, and in what ways is it bad?

The image of Christ, calling us to do good in verses 37-41 is motivating. We can do good, we can do better, and we can do great today because we will listen for his voice. What things will you do in his name today? Remember that repentance and learning from mistakes is also a part of hearing his voice.

Day 143, Alma 5:43-52

What did Alma do in verses 43-47 to make sure he didn't give a talk about things other people have said? Which doctrines and principles have you done that with, and which ones do you feel as if you still need to do that with?

Alma mentioned he was going to speak of "things which are to come" (:44). So, what did he say would happen in verses 48-50?

Why do you think the message from the spirit so often is to repent (:50-52)? What have you done to make sure you view repentance as a blessing and not as a burden? Why do you think the symbol of the axe at the foot of the tree is great to help us understand repentance?

Day 144, Alma 5:53-6:8

In Alma 5:53-56, notice how often the word "persist" is used. Is there something you are doing that, if you persist in doing it, will lead to your unhappiness and possible destruction?

In Alma 5:57-61, look for what determines if a name is written or blotted out? Why do you think those names can't remain mingled like they do on earth?

How was order established in Alma 6:1-4? What blessing and protection did this order add to the church and to the lives of its members?

Why do you think it is important that people can gather together, and why do you think it is important that they do gather together (6:5-6)?

Day 145, Alma 7:1-13

In verses 1-6, we see the differences between the cities of Zarahemla and Gideon. Because of their previous spiritual preparation, the people of

Gideon are prepared for greater spiritual teachings. In what ways has preparing yourself before a meeting, talk, or lesson made a significant difference in what you were then able to receive?

In verses 7-13, Alma begins to explain the mission of Jesus Christ and the role that His Atonement will play in everyone's life. Verses 11-13 drastically expand the traditional view of what the Atonement was meant for—not just for sin and death, but for much, much more our Savior suffered for us. If you will look for the word "that" in these verses it will help you identify these other reasons. Which of these purposes of the Atonement can be helpful to you this week?

In those same verses, notice the phrase "take upon him." What does this phrase suggest about Christ's willingness and overall experience?

Sometimes people will try to use verse 10 to discredit the Book of Mormon because Alma didn't say Jesus would be born in Bethlehem, but instead said Jerusalem. The people Alma is talking to have not lived in the Middle East for hundreds of years. They know that Lehi and Nephi came from Jerusalem. This is a term to describe their homeland. Just because Alma didn't mention Bethlehem, a city less than five miles away from Jerusalem, doesn't mean Joseph Smith made up the Book of Mormon. Likewise, because few people in Utah know where Salina is, I say it is near Richfield. You have probably used this same technique also. In the end, how might this actually be evidence in favor of the authenticity of the Book of Mormon?

Day 146, Alma 7:14-27

Yesterday, Alma outlined one of the greatest sections of verses regarding the purpose of the Atonement. Today, he will speak about why we need an Atonement and how to use it. On a piece of paper, make two columns. Title one: "Why we need the Atonement." Title the other: "How to use the Atonement." Then, as you read verses 14-27, make notes on what you learn under each heading.

We also learned yesterday that Christ suffered so that He could better understand and help us. We can begin to understand and feel how Christ and our Heavenly Parents feel by applying the Atonement and developing their attributes. We are asked to take action and repent/change because we stopped using or being one or more of the qualities described in verses 23-24. Which of those qualities needs to be activated in your life?

Do you really believe that this transformation is possible in your own life through the power of the Atonement?

Day 147, Alma 8:1-17

Both in Zarahemla and in Melek, Alma established the "order of the church" (:1) and the "holy order of God" (:4). Why do you think it is important to have order? What are the blessings of having order?

What evidence is there that Alma was a good missionary in verses 6-15, even though he was not successful? What factors led to the people rejecting the message of Alma?

I love the fact that Alma didn't feel like there was an angel close by while he was walking away from Ammonihah (:14). What might that teach us about the ministering of angels in our own lives?

What does verses 15 teach us about effort and results?

Why do you think the same angel that appeared to correct Alma now appears to comfort him?

According to verses 16-17, what would have happened to Ammonihah, and maybe to the Nephite people, if Alma didn't go back and preach?

Day 148, Alma 8:18-9:6

Yesterday, Alma was told to return to the city of Ammonihah. What impresses you about how Alma responded in Alma 8:18? What thing would the Lord like you to respond to with the same attention?

What preparations had heaven been making to get Amulek ready for Alma? Do you think anyone ever joins this church without the preparation of heaven? What miracles and mercies do you think heaven will prepare for you today?

Alma 8:31-32 mentions the power that was given to both Alma and Amulek. As you read today's section, look for what they do to prepare for and obtain this power. What preparations does the Lord want you to make so that he can bestow greater power upon you?

Day 149, Alma 9:7-18

As you read today's section, you may want to mark the words "forgotten," "not remembered," and "remember." What do you think is the connection between faithfulness and remembering? What do you think the connection is between forgetting, false traditions, and being cut off?

What patterns and practices do you have in your life that help you remember Heavenly Father, Jesus Christ, and what they have done for you?

Today's section also spoke a lot about judgment and accountability. When is it a blessing to be held more accountable?

Day 150, Alma 9:19-34

As you read Alma's words to the people of Ammonihah, consider how you would finish each of the following statements:

God will destroy people if they. . .

God would rather have his people destroyed than. . .

To help people avoid destruction God. . .

People who are destroying their own lives should. . .

I will make sure that I don't destroy my life by. . .

In verses 20-22, look for the spirits, gifts, and blessings given to the Nephites. How do the current blessings and privileges you have compare to those given to the Nephites? What differences do they make to you and others?

Day 151, Alma 10:1-16

In verses 1-6, look for what we can learn about Amulek and his history.

What does verse 6 teach you about the Lord's desire to rescue his children? When was the last time the Lord called you to do something—not just to do your calling, but to bless the life of someone else?

In verses 7-11, look for the effect Alma had on Amulek's family and testimony.

How have the living prophets been a blessings to your family and testimony?

Who are the other holy men and women that the Lord has sent into your life to bless you? Who has the Lord sent you to bless?

Day 152, Alma 10:17-34

How are prophets, leaders, and mothers able to know and perceive the thoughts of others? Check out footnote 17b for more information.

What does Amulek say in verses 22-23 about the role the righteous play in societies that are making bad choices? The way that we live will either help or hurt not just us and our families, but also our communities. Speaking of the power of righteous families, President Dieter F. Uchtdorf said, "One righteous family can change a city, and ten righteous families can change a whole country." (Dieter F. Uchtdorf. Kyiv, Ukraine conference, June 6, 2009)

Read verses 25-27, and 32, then finish this sentence: "It is not politics, lawyers, and judges that Amulek warns against, but. . ."

In verse 30 we learn that the lawyers, "put it into their hearts that they should remember these things against him."

Day 153, Alma 11:1-25

The money talk in verses 1-19 is all to help us understand the amount of the bribe that Zeezrom offers to Amulek (:22). Six onties is equal to about six weeks of pay.

The temptations and bribes offered to us to deny our belief and faith are not always as obvious as this. They come as we are invited to think, feel, and act contrary to the Holy Ghost. Notice how Amulek uses the Spirit as his guide in verse 22. Today, will you choose to have fewer moments when you think, feel, and act contrary to the Holy Ghost?

In verse 25, Amulek reveals that Zeezrom's intent never was to give him the promised bribe. In what ways does that mirror the offers that are made to us daily regarding our faith and belief?

Day 154, Alma 11:26-46

In verses 26-41, Zeezrom tries to trap Amulek by confusing the Godhead and using the word "in" instead of "from."

In verses 34-37, what does Amulek say to explain why Christ can't save people "in" their sins, but only from them? What sin do you need to be saved from?

The confusion that is sometimes found while studying verses 38-39 can be cleared up if you add the words: "of creation and the covenant" right after "Eternal Father" in verse 38. Amulek is answering the question that Zeezrom should have asked. Amulek knows that Jesus and Heavenly Father are two separate people (:32-33). Amulek is also familiar with the teachings of King Benjamin, who taught how Christ can also become our Father (Mosiah 5:7). This explains why the righteous are called Christ's people and the wicked are left as though there never was an Atonement, except for the blessing of resurrection (:40-41).

Speaking of the resurrection, Amulek now gives us some great verses on the purpose, participants, and power of this doctrine in verses 42-45. What did you discover about the resurrection?

Day 155, Alma 12:1-19

Alma and Amulek didn't fall for Zeezrom's trap because they listened to the spirit. We don't have to fall for the traps that are laid to ensnare us if we listen to the spirit (:1-7).

God is really good at keeping secrets and mysteries. He does not give them away cheap. What does Alma teach Zeezrom in verses 8-11 about how to obtain the mysteries and secrets of God? If God is careful about sharing some things, then why do you think we should also be careful with how we treat the mysteries He has given to us?

Because of the resurrection, we will all receive immortal bodies and stand to be judged before the Lord. What do verses 12-15 say about what can condemn us, how to avoid condemnation, and our wishes if we don't?

Physical death is when the body and the spirit are separated. What is spiritual death, according to verses 16-18, and how is it similar or different from physical death?

Day 156, Alma 12:20-33

Not knowing the Plan of Salvation, Antionah is confused by the doctrine of resurrection and how people can live forever when God made sure Adam and Eve couldn't partake of the tree of life after the Fall. To help clear up this misunderstanding, Alma explains the importance that death and mortal life play in the Plan of Salvation in verses 22-27.

How would you complete the following statement? "Death is necessary because . . ."

If this life is to prepare to return to God, then what preparations will you make today?

In verses 28-33, look for what assistance and help God provided to his children to help them in their probationary life. What is God doing to help prepare you to live with him again?

We, like Adam and Eve, all chose to leave God and live a mortal life. According to verse 31 how does this Fall help us become more like the Gods?

Now, complete this statement: "The Fall is necessary because . . ."

Day 157, Alma 12:34-13:9

Find the phrases "my rest" and "rest of the Lord" in Alma 12:34-37. You may want to mark them. We know that God is not lazy. So what do you think "the rest of the Lord" means? What do we learn from these verses about how to and how not to obtain the rest of the Lord?

What does Alma 13:1-9 teach us about why people receive the priesthood and the blessings of the priesthood?

What does Alma 13:1-9 teach us about what people are supposed to do after they have received the priesthood and the blessings thereof?

What does it mean that those who hold the priesthood are "ordained after the order of his Son" (Alma 13:1-2, and 7-8)? What does this mean about what they are supposed to become? According to Alma 13:2, why are men to become like Jesus Christ? What do you feel you should do to live your life more "after the order of the Son of God?"

Day 158, Alma 13:10-31

Included in the footnotes of his October 2013 General Conference talk, "Power in the Priesthood" Elder Neil L. Andersen quoted Elder M. Russell Ballard: "Why are men ordained to priesthood offices and not women? President Gordon B. Hinckley explained that it was the Lord, not man, 'who designated that men in His Church should hold the priesthood' and that it was also the Lord who endowed women with 'capabilities to round out this great and marvelous organization, which is the Church and kingdom of God' ("Women of the Church," Ensign, November 1996, 70). When all is said and done, the Lord has not revealed why He has organized His Church as He has." (M. Russell Ballard, "Let Us Think Straight" (BYU Campus Education Week devotional, Aug. 20, 2013) When you get an Apostle quoting an Apostle quoting a prophet, that is a good quote. We don't know why men hold the priesthood, but we know that the men who do are to become the best examples of Christ. Search verses (:14-19) for ways in which Melchizedek did the things that Christ would have done.

Yesterday's section spoke of entering into the rest of the Lord. Today's section mentions this idea and additional four more times (:12-13, 16, and 29). In summary, what we have learned is that to obtain the rest of the Lord, we must become like the Lord and do the work of the Lord. In what ways have ordinances, priesthood, callings, commandments, and meetings all helped you to better do those things?

In addition to the rest of the Lord, we are warned against wresting the scriptures in verse 20. What is the difference between rest and wrest? How are you preventing this attitude in yourself and others?

Day 159, Alma 14:1-13

Some of the most painful moments in life come when we are ridiculed, misunderstood, or even injured by those who we are honestly trying to help. In today's section, you will see the increasing torment of Alma and Amulek by those they are trying to help. Sometimes we may think it would be better not to love people as much as God does. Surely, it would be easier to retire to a beach paradise and read great books and eat fabulous food. But, we came here to become like God in how we think, feel, and act. That includes loving and hurting like God does, and the pain of God is always caused by the choices of others.

Why does God allow wicked people to hurt the good in ways that seem unrecoverable? Where are the miracles and delivery? What answers does Alma give to these heartrending questions in verses 11-13?

How can these verses and the lessons they teach be of use to you and the situations that you're facing right now?

Day 160, Alma 14:14-29

Look for how the captors of Alma and Amulek misunderstood the power of God and His servants. How were each of these misunderstandings corrected? Why do you think people demand proof of the power of God and His servants? What evidences and experiences have you had that demonstrate the power of God and His authorized servants?

Notice the responses of Alma and Amulek to the accusatory questions in verses 17-19. When would this be an appropriate reply instead of following the counsel of Peter to "be ready always to give an answer to every man that asketh you a reason of the hope that is in you" (1 Peter 3:15)?

After many days their faith in Christ broke their bands, and he will also break ours.

Day 161, Alma 15:1-12

In the previous chapter, these people and others were hurt because of their faith. Now, look for what happens to them because of their faith and belief.

"Believest thou in the power of Christ unto salvation?" (:6)

What miracle or blessing have you experienced because of your belief? For "all things are possible to him that believeth" (Mark 9:23).

I don't know of anything that causes more pain and grief than the conviction through the Holy Ghost that I have sinned and deeply offended God. Zeezrom knows this pain (:3-5), and deliverance only comes through belief in the Savior's Atonement. Christ delivers us from all types of burnings, including those of the last chapter that consumed those who believed.

Day 162, Alma 15:13-16:11

In Alma 15:13-18, look for what Alma does to minister to large groups of people as well as the one. Here are two quotes to help us in our personal ministry to others:

"I have not come to England to be in this meeting. Now, I'm here and I love this, and we are doing important things, but that's not why I'm here. While I'm in England the Lord sent me to find a one. And along the way I get to participate in a bunch of meetings, and maybe some good will be done. But, the Keys of the Kingdom were sent here to find a one. You don't talk to a congregation you talk to assembled ones. So just go get one, who will get one, who will get one, and that is how it works, and that is how you establish the Kingdom, and that is how ultimately thousands come." (Reaching Many "Ones" in England Conference).

"When I was a young man, I served as counselor to a wise district president in the Church. He tried to teach me. One of the things I remember wondering about was this advice he gave: 'When you meet someone, treat them as if they were in serious trouble, and you will be right more than half the time.'" (Elder Henry B. Eyring. "In the Strength of the Lord", Ensign, May 2004)

In Alma 16:1-11, we will see the destruction and desolation of Ammoniah. Let's look at the example of Ammonihah to learn how you destroy a city, family, or an individual life. They not only did wicked things, but they removed all individuals and influences that were good from their lives (Alma 14:7-9). They never said sorry for anything they did, for they "did not believe in the repentance of their sins" (Alma 15:15). Can you imagine what it would be like to be in a family with someone like that? We can avoid destruction and desolation from coming upon our own families as we seek to be surrounded by righteous people and influences, and keep our hearts soft through sincere and frequent repentance.

What does the story in Alma 16:4-8 teach us about how to reclaim those who have become captured or lost?

Day 163, Alma 16:12-21

Today's section ends with "the Lord pouring out his blessings upon the people" (:21). As you read, look for what they did to deserve blessings to be poured out upon them.

In order to receive the gospel, why do you think it is important to have both the heart and the mind prepared by the Lord (:16-17)? Who do you know that the Lord has been preparing? The only way to discover the preparedness of a heart or mind is to make an invitation and see how they respond (D&C 29:7). Now, let's discover the condition of your heart and mind. Will you make an inspired invitation to the person that you believe the Lord has been preparing?

The gospel invited us to do several good things, but there are also things that we are against. Why are we against those things listed in verse 18?

Day 164, Alma 17:1-17

God desires His people to be powerful teachers, preachers, and missionaries. He has not sent us to be weak in our teaching, or inviting. We must, however, pay the price. The sons of Mosiah have been on a mission for fourteen years. They have learned how to have access to the power of God. As you read today's verses, search for the things that allowed them to be powerful preachers of righteousness.

Which of those simple things do you feel you could do more diligently? How will you will be able to unlock the power of God in your own life, and in the lives of others?

How could the sons of Mosiah find comfort in verse 10 when they were given the information in verse 11? How might we take comfort if we feel we are living in the middle of verse 11?

Look at what is said about the Lamanites in verses 14-16. Have you ever felt the same way about a home teaching or visiting teaching assignment? What allows a person to see people differently than the rest of the world sees them? In what ways do our invitations, visits, and attempts demonstrate faith, hope, and charity?

Day 165, Alma 17:18-31

Ammon has come among the Lamanites to teach them the gospel. He is bold, but also careful in his approach. As you read, notice all the places where you think Ammon was extremely wise in how he handled the situation. What did you find?

Doing nothing doesn't make a person wise. In what ways will you be wise, careful, and deliberate in sharing the gospel with others this week?

Day 166, Alma 17:31-18:7

In Alma 17:31-39, what lessons can we learn about leadership and our responsibility to care for others from the example of how Ammon shepherded the King's flocks?

What does Alma 17:35 show us about the effect parents can have on their children?

The Lamanites thought Ammon was weak and that he would be easy to kill. Throughout the years many people have had that same opinion of the Church. What principles, promises, and comparisons can you see between Ammon defending the flocks from robbers, and people seeking to attack and destroy the Church (Alma 17:33-37)?

Look for the different ways that testimony was shared in Alma 17:39-18:7. What impact did these testimonies or witnesses have on King Lamoni?

Day 167, Alma 18:8-23

King Lamoni was astonished at how well Ammon did his job. "Never, never underestimate the spiritual value of doing temporal things well for those whom you serve" (Henry B. Eyring. "The Book of Mormon Will Change Your Life" [CES symposium on the Book of Mormon, Aug. 17, 1990], 7).

Look for places where Ammon used these key principles of teaching as he taught Lamoni: teach by the spirit, teach people and not lessons, ask inspired questions, don't be afraid of silence, listen, seek and expect revelation. How can you use the example of Ammon to become a more powerful teacher?

Day 168, Alma 18:24-19:11

In Alma 18:24-39, we will continue to see Ammon demonstrate his teaching skills through the following: build on common ground, accommodate your teaching to the level of the student, bear testimony, ask questions to check understanding and belief, teach from the scriptures, share stories, relate personal experiences, and teach basic doctrines of the Plan of Salvation. Which of these teaching principles are you good at, and which ones could you improve on?

The impact of Ammon's teaching was powerful. King Lamoni cried out for mercy and then fell to the ground. After two days, there is discussion about the state of his body and smell. When Ammon is approached about the condition of the King, he is not worried because he knows what is happening and describes it in Alma 19:6. Normally people are not knocked to the ground for days when this happens. How does a person usually go through the change described in Alma 19:6?

In Alma 19:10, Ammon declared that the faith of King Lamoni's wife exceeded that of the Nephites. In Alma 19:1-11, look for all the places that she showed this exceeding faith. How will you show more faith today?

Day 169, Alma 19:12-21

In today's section, look for how the faith and choices of Ammon ripple down to bless others in their faith and choices. When has someone's example or testimony influenced you for good?

The scriptures describe the spiritual experience of King Lamoni, his wife, and their servants as being "overpowered" (:13-14). When was the last time you felt the influence of the Spirit in a powerful way?

We do not get many named women in The Book of Mormon. Abish is one of these rare named women. What amazing things do we learn about her in verses 16-17? What things can we learn from her in verses 16-17?

Day 170, Alma 19:22-36

As a parent, how do verses 22-23 increase your desire to plead in prayer for your children? As a child, how do these verses build your gratitude for blessings that were paid for by the faith of your parents?

King Lamoni's wife delivers a powerful and simple testimony about what Christ can save us from and fill us with in verses 29-30.

Watch for how the word "many" is used in verses 30-36 to draw our attention to several important things that we can learn.

In verse 36, Mormon wants to make sure that we don't miss an important truth, so he uses one of his well-known "we see" statements. When it comes to remembering the story of Ammon, we usually remember the arms being cut off but, according to this statement, what is another thing that we are to learn from the story of Ammon?

Day 171, Alma 20:1-18

In verses 1-7, we learn that the Lord will direct us to places and people who need our help if we follow the promptings that we receive. While this principle is true, we usually have to ask a question of the Lord first. The question that helps me get this type of revelation is, "Where do you want me to go, and who do you want me to minister to?"

When have you seen someone accept the gospel and reject the false traditions of their fathers, like King Lamoni in verses 8-15?

Do you think Ammon was telling the truth to King Lamoni's father in verses 17-18, or was he just trying to scare him? If Ammon knew you, would there be anything he would warn you of that could cost you your soul?

Day 172, Alma 20:19-21:4

In what ways might we see examples of Jesus in the actions of Ammon? Consider the ability to take and spare a life, deliver prisoners, and receive, reject, and bestow kingdoms.

King Lamoni's father was "astonished exceedingly" by the great love Ammon had for his son (:26). When have you been astonished exceedingly by the love of someone?

Ammon was "exceedingly sorrowful" because of the condition of his brothers when they were finally delivered (:29). To be affected by the hardships of others is an attribute of the Savior. Can you imagine Jesus saying the same things in verse 29 about the circumstances of many around the world?

Day 173, Alma 21:5-23

Questions are the key to learning and receiving revelation. As we begin to hear the missionary travels of Aaron, look at the questions that were asked of him by an Amalekite in verses 5-6. Why is the intent of our questions more important than the question itself? What questions do you have about gospel issues that may require you to change your intent so you can get better answers from heaven?

Sometimes the people with whom we try to share the gospel are uninterested and maybe even rude. Notice how Aaron and his fellow missionaries handled some of these difficult circumstances in verses 7-17. What principles from those verses could help us when we find ourselves interacting with those who may not be interested or even hostile to the gospel?

The people of King Lamoni became "zealous for keeping the commandments of God" (:23). Look at what Ammon and King Lamoni did in verses 18-23 that developed this quality in the people. Was there anything that they did that you feel you could do in your own home that would bring about similar results?

Day 174, Alma 22:1-14

Yesterday, we mentioned the importance of intent with asking questions. Today, you will see how King Lamoni's father has been "troubled in the mind" because of what he has heard (:3). As you read verses 1-11, look for evidence that his intent was sincere.

At some point in your gospel study or while visiting with someone, you will come across things that trouble your mind and maybe even your heart. It is important to remember to ask questions about the things that trouble you, asking with faith and a sincere intent to learn. There is nothing wrong with having questions or even being troubled. Do what Lamoni's father did: Ponder and wait, ask someone, study from the scriptures, put things into the context of the Plan of Salvation, and understand the basic doctrines better. You don't need to be afraid of any question about the gospel. What questions do you have that you feel you could pursue asking and wrestling with in faith, rather than doubt?

In verses 12-14, look for how the doctrine of creation, the Fall, and redemption through Christ are connected.

Day 175, Alma 22:15-26

As you read verses 15-18, look for what Lamoni's father wanted, what he was willing to give up in order to obtain it, and what Aaron told him he would have to give up. It is not a matter of what would you give up, but what God wants you to give up. What sin does God want you to surrender or have rooted out of you?

What choices does Aaron have to make for public relation reasons in verses 19-26? We know that we are accountable to God, but why is it important to be aware of how others are viewing us?

After the King was converted, what impact was he then able to have on his family, and others (:23-26)? Have you done enough personal study and prayer today that you will be able to "minister," "administer," and "pacify" your family and others?

Day 176, Alma 22:27-23:7

There have been several books, videos, articles, websites, and even organizations devoted to the discovery of the Book of Mormon geography. Little details found throughout the text of the book, like those in Alma 22:27-35, give us a few clues, but no specific locations. As fun as this stuff is, the official position of the Church is that the location of where the Book of Mormon took place is unknown. Throughout the life of the Book of Mormon, several people, including church leaders, have tried to pin down the location. In the early days of the Church, the belief was that the Book of Mormon land was all of North and South America. More recently decades scholars have theorized that the area would have been only a few hundred miles wide and long, relatively small. This size of area accounts for increased difficulty in securing archeological evidence of the Book of Mormon, especially in a tropical climate.

As you read Alma 23:1-7, consider this question. Why is it advantageous for the modern day Church to work directly and openly with governments?

Why would the last few lines of Alma 23:6 be a good indicator of missionary success?

Day 177, Alma 23:8-24:6

Some missionaries write down the names of those they help convert. Look for what Ammon, Aaron, and others could have written down according to Alma 23:8-15.

Often we use the word "anti" to mean opposite or against, but sometimes we use it to mirror or resemble something, like the word antichrist. So are the Anti-Nephi-Lehies against Nephi and Lehi, or are they trying to mirror them? They have changed their lives, so they want to change their names. What insights does that give us about name changes we go through?

Notice how the two groups of people in Alma 24:1-6 respond to people who have different beliefs and values than them.

Day 178, Alma 24:7-19

In verses 7-10, look for what the King is thankful. For what do you have to be thankful to God?

Which one of the following phrases do you think best describes the point that the King is trying to make in verses 10-15: Sin is painful, be grateful for forgiveness, repentance is difficult, the Atonement is powerful?

In verses 15-19, we will see that the Anti-Nephi-Lehies hide their weapons in the earth. Why do you think they hide them at the depth they did? We all have weapons that we use to harm and hurt others. Sometimes my impulsive nature to have fun and be funny causes me to say and do things that harm others. When this happens, I can feel the Lord calling for me to bury this weapon deeper through meaningful repentance. What does the Lord want you to bury? This is hard because, if you ask, he will tell you. Ultimately, knowing these truths will bless your life.

Day 179, Alma 24:19-25:6

As Mormon is abridging the plates, he will sometimes include a statement like "thus we see." Speaking about such statements, President Henry B. Eyring said "What went before does not prove the conclusion the way the world looks for evidence or logic. What went before is what someone with spiritual sight will observe and then say, 'Oh, yes, now I see that.' And then follows, after the 'thus we see,' what that someone would see. When I understood that, I realized how gracious the word we is in that phrase 'and thus we see.' The writer was saying, 'I include you with me among those who see.' Ever since then, each time I read the words 'we see' in the Book of Mormon, I have felt a warm burning for two reasons: First, the feeling of being included as a seeker and a believer by the writer. . .; and second, I have felt the burning that tells me that the thing the writer could see was true." (Henry B. Eyring. "And Thus We See": Helping A Student In A Moment of Doubt. Address to CES Religious Educators, 5 February 1993).

We have three such statements in today's section (Alma 24:19, 27, and 30). Which of these statements is most impressed upon your mind after reading the story found in Alma 24:19-30?

In Alma 16:1-11, we read about the destruction of Ammonihah. Now in Alma 25:1-2, we learn why the Lamanites attacked that city. Another great connection is found in Alma 25:5b which speaks about a prophecy of Abinadi being fulfilled.

Day 180, Alma 25:7-26:9

In Alma 25:7-12, we get more about the prophecy of Abinadi being fulfilled. In your lifetime, what prophecies have you seen fulfilled that the prophets have spoken?

In Alma 26, we will get one of the greatest missionary reports from one of the greatest missionaries of all time. Look in Alma 26:1-4 and Alma 26:5-9, and come up with a lesson we can learn from each.

How does the following quote from President Dieter F. Uchtdorf help us understand what it means to be an instrument in God's hands (:3)? "I once owned a pen that I loved to use during my career as an airline captain. By simply turning the shaft, I could choose one of four colors. The pen did not complain when I wanted to use red ink instead of blue. It did not say to me, 'I would rather not write after 10:00 p.m., in heavy fog, or at high altitudes.' The pen did not say, 'Use me only for important documents, not for the daily mundane tasks.' With greatest reliability it performed every task I needed, no matter how important or insignificant. It was always ready to serve" ("Pride and Priesthood", Ensign Nov. 2010).

To help us better understand Alma 26:5-9, Elder Bednar has taught "The sheaves in this analogy represent newly baptized members of the Church. The garners are the holy temples" ("Honorably Hold a Name and Standing," Ensign, May 2009). What can this passage teach us about the temple and its power?

Day 181, Alma 26:10-22

Today we will continue with Ammon's great missionary report. Look for a significant truth that you can learn from each of these blocks of scripture 11-12, 13-16, 17-20, and 21-22.

What do you think the word "snatched" in verse 17 can teach us about the speed with which God can redeem us when we are ready?

What do verses 21-22 teach us about how to increase revelation, and what we can do with that revelation?

Day 182, Alma 26:23-37

This is our third and final day discovering principles from this amazing missionary discourse by Ammon. Try to discover a principle in each of the following groupings: 23-26, 27-30, 31-34, 35, and 36-37. I know this is very similar to the last two days, but if you are thoughtful and careful you will discover some wonderful truths. For instance, mark the word "mindful" in verses 36-37. According to these verses, of whom is God mindful? Do you believe that God is mindful of you? What evidence have you had in your life that God is indeed mindful of you?

Day 183, Alma 27:1-15

Look for the different directions love has grown among these people in verse 4. In the last month, how has your church association and service deepened your love for others?

In verses 5-14, we will learn a lesson that we already know but will benefit us to review. When faced with a problem, they studied it out, counseled about it, decided on a possible direction, and inquired of the Lord. What problem do you need to run through this pattern right now?

Day 184, Alma 27:16-28:8

As you read Alma 27:16-19, you may want to mark the words "joy," "joyful," and "happiness." The sons of Mosiah had found tremendous happiness in their service. What joy and happiness have you found in your church membership, callings, and service?

The prophet Joseph Smith taught, "Happiness is the object and design of our existence; and will be the end thereof, if we pursue the path that leads to it; and this path is virtue, uprightness, faithfulness, holiness, and keeping all the commandments of God" (Teachings of the Prophet Joseph Smith, sel. Joseph Fielding Smith [1976], 255–56). Look for how Ammon and his people qualified for this promised happiness in Alma 27:25-30. Was there anything that they were doing that you could start doing, so that the Lord might increase your joy and happiness?

New converts and those returning to activity are in great need of friendly faces, welcoming hands, and love from the congregation. Look for what the Nephites did to make sure these new converts felt loved and protected in Alma 27:20-24 and 28:1-8. What would the Lord have you do to help those who are new and returning in your ward?

Day 185, Alma 28:9-29:9

After a time of fierce war and suffering, Mormon pointed out lessons he hoped we would learn by using several "thus we see" statements in Alma 28:11-14. Which of these lessons do you think are also applicable to the time in which we now live?

In Alma 29:1-9, Alma goes through a miraculous process that ends in holy contentment. What does Alma teach us about desires, allotment, and contentment in these verses?

Day 186, Alma 29:10-30:11

In Alma 29:10-17, notice how many times Alma mentions that he experiences joy through the success of his brethren. Why do you think the ability to rejoice when others are successful is an important part of discipleship?

As Alma is recalling the great things that have happened in his ministry, it occurs to him that the "same God" who delivered ancient Israel, is the "same God" that has called and blessed him (29:12-13). What difference does it make when we realize that all blessings flow to people from the "same God?" How has the "same God" that delivered Israel and blessed Alma assisted you in the last few days?

Tomorrow, we will learn more about this antichrist, but today I want you to look for why religious freedom was an important part of the Nephite legal system in Alma 30:1-10. Over the last few years, we have received a consistent message from living prophets about religious freedom. An example of this effort can be found in the new "Religious Freedom" video series that has been produced by The Church of Jesus Christ of Latter-day Saints. This series was introduced by Elder Von. G. Keetch of the Seventy, while speaking at a Brigham Young University-Idaho devotional. For more information you can click on the "Religious Freedom" icon on the Gospel Library app or search "Religious Freedom" on lds.org.

Day 187, Alma 30:12-28

President Ezra Taft Benson said: "The Book of Mormon exposes the enemies of Christ. It confounds false doctrines and lays down contention. (See 2 Ne. 3:12.) It fortifies the humble followers of Christ against the evil designs, strategies, and doctrines of the devil in our day. The type of apostates in the Book of Mormon are similar to the type we have today. God, with his infinite foreknowledge, so molded the Book of Mormon that we might see the error and know how to combat false educational, political, religious, and philosophical concepts of our time" (Teachings of the Presidents of the Church: Ezra Taft Benson, 132). Korihor is one of those enemies. His numerous teachings are also among those enemies. As you read today's section, look at each of Korihor's teachings and consider if it is still being promoted by some in our time.

The Church has a really good video that depicts our story for the next few days. It is called "All Things Denote There Is a God." You can search for it by that name or under "Alma and Korihor video."

Without a knowledge of the plan and a witness from the Holy Ghost, Korihor's teachings are logical. Because they are logical, members sometimes feel confused when they encounter such teachings and ideas in the world. Take the time to examine each of Korihor's teachings and you will find that each is based on incorrect knowledge about the Plan of Salvation or a basic doctrine. I would invite you not to let those who do not understand the gospel and the plan—or who have not had the spiritual experiences that you have had—to "interrupt your rejoicings" (:22).

Day 188, Alma 30:29-49

One of Korihor's claims is that Church leaders lie to obtain wealth (:31). This is also a current criticism of the modern Church. Look how Alma responds in verses 32-35. Alma speaks of the joy of teaching and preaching the gospel, as well as the joy from living the gospel. How have you experienced each of these joys recently? Do you feel that you have been deceived into experiencing that joy? In the modern Church, the General Authorities and others receive a living allowance depending on their circumstances. These living allowances are paid for by the business efforts of the Church and not the tithing of members. Most local church leaders are unpaid for their efforts.

In verses 36-44, look for all the things that bolstered Alma's faith and convinced him there was a God. Why do you think that not everyone is convinced that there is a God according to the list that Alma cites? Which things on Alma's list have you also experienced for yourself?

Divine signs are tricky (:45-49). If you believe, you have probably experienced several things you would consider to be divine signs. For a person who does not believe, signs are often demanded and seldom recognized. Are you more concerned about the signs you send to God or the signs He sends to you?

Day 189, Alma 30:50-60

When you interact with people who are openly hostile against the Savior and His Church, don't expect the Lord to seal their mouth or make them dumb if destroying the person is not the best option. What do you think the Lord desires of us when we are faced with such situations?

Verse 53 is terrifying when you consider that the Apostle Paul also warned that the devil could appear as an angel of light (2 Corinthians 11:14). Luckily, we have prophets who teach us patterns to protect us, like Joseph Smith did in D&C 129:1-9. When have you been able to detect the deception of the devil by the help of the prophets or the Holy Ghost?

Verse 53 is also a great warning about being careful of what we are taught and what we teach.

There are a couple of great scriptures that define who God is and what he desires for us, like Moses 1:39 and 2 Nephi 26:24. There are also a couple of key verses to describe Satan. One of those is found in Alma 30:60. When have you felt your loving Father in Heaven supporting you?

Day 190, Alma 31:1-23

In verses 1-4, look for how Alma felt about those who had separated themselves from the Nephites and the Church.

Verse 5 is a summary of the entire book of Alma. We just spent the last 31 chapters learning about the power of the word, with chapters 43-63 focusing on the power of the sword. In an effort to reclaim and to help people change, why do you think the word of God is more powerful than force or other techniques?

When did you gain a greater desire to do what was right because of the scriptures or the teachings of a church leader?

As you read verses 12-23, consider how you might protect your worship and prayers from becoming like that of the Zoramites. Why do you think it is important to have meaningful prayers and to worship often?

Day 191, Alma 31:24-38

Yesterday, we looked at the prayer of the Zoramites. Today, we will get the counter prayer of Alma. Not only was Alma's prayer different, how might his feelings have been different when he was done?

Who do you need to cry unto God for?

Notice that Alma prayed for the Zoramites and his fellow missionaries, but he also prayed for himself. He didn't ask God to change the circumstances that he was in; instead he pleaded with God to change him and increase his capacity to meet the challenges of his circumstances. Every problem and challenge we face is an opportunity to seek, plead, and cry for Christlike character and attributes. What attribute of Christ do you need to pray for to help you in the circumstances that you are in?

Day 192, Alma 32:1-20

After reading today's section complete each one of these following phrases:

Being poor sometimes. . .
Humility sometimes. . .
True humility and penitence always. . .

In your own life, can you tell the difference between when you are truly humble and when you are compelled into humility?

What does God want you to surrender to Him and to start or stop doing "without stubbornness" (:16)?

What do verses 9-11 teach us about worship? Is there a way in which these verses and their meaning could be taken out of context?

Day 193, Alma 32:21-33

According to the message of verse 21, what are some things in which you can have faith?

What do verses 26-33 say about how to grow, strengthen, and perfect our faith?

What are some gospel concepts that you have experimented with and have felt this promised growth?

What are some gospel concepts that might need some experimenting?

In what ways is Alma 32:28 similar to Moroni 10:5 and the promises made there?

Day 194, Alma 32:33-33:11

Sometimes, people are confused that members of the Church use the word "know" in their testimonies. With what we learned from Alma's experiment discussion yesterday, and in Alma 32:33-35, how can members claim that they know things are true when they testify?

Faith to know that something is true is different than the faith to do good things. The faith to do miracles is also different from the faith to receive your calling and election, or secure your exhalation. Read Alma 32:36-43 and discover what makes the difference between those whose faith flounders and those whose faith flourishes. What marvelous things will you do today because of your faith?

Notice that the word, through faith, has grown from seed to sprout to tree, and then bears fruit (Alma 32:28, 30, and 37). We are not just developing one tree, but each truth of the gospel has the chance to produce wonderful fruits in our lives. We are after a gospel orchard. Don't get caught up comparing your orchard to others; just grow each principle in its season by using faith in the Atonement. Look for how Alma gives this same type of counsel in Alma 33:1-11.

Day 195, Alma 33:12-23

Since the publishing of the Book of Mormon, critics have sought to dismiss it as illegitimate through many different means. One of those has revolved around certain names like: Zenos and Zenock and the lack of evidence for their existence. Other names used to be included in this group like Alma and Mahijah. Until the Book of Mormon, Alma was thought to have only been a female name. This information was used to attack the belief of many members. In 1961 an ancient document in the Palestine region was found, by Professor Yigael that deeded land to a man named Alma. When people attack what we don't know, do not let that change what we do know.

Answer each of the questions in verses 12-14.

Look for what each of the following prophets teaches us about Jesus and his Atonement: Zenos in verse 13, Zenock in verse 16, Moses in verses 19-22, and Alma in verse 23. Pick one and ponder on it. Consider how moving and insightful it really is.

Many of Moses' people died because they would not look at or to a symbolic representation of Jesus. Will you look to Him today for healing and strength?

Day 196, Alma 34:1-16

In verses 1-7, Amulek shares that there have been several testimonies given about Jesus Christ. Then, in verse 8, Amulek shares his own testimony and witness of Jesus. At this point in your life, what would your testimony about the need and importance for Christ include?

As you study verses 9-14, look for what they say about why Jesus, the Son of God, a God himself, would have to perform the Atonement?

The Law of Justice: For every obedience to the law there is a blessing which produces joy. For every disobedience of the law there is punishment which produces suffering.

The Law of Mercy: Someone else can suffer, if they are able, and if they are willing.

With an understanding of these two laws, substitute these definitions as you study verses 15-16.

Day 197, Alma 34:17-41

I believe that the act of prayer truly requires faith, and because of that, prayer has the capability to increase our faith tremendously. I also believe that thoughtless, checklist prayers have the power to destroy our faith and belief in God. Watch for the attitude of prayer that is presented by Amulek in verses 17-27. I love the idea in verse 26 that prayer is a pouring out of our souls. Will you continue in your effort to say heartfelt prayers?

"The efficacy of our prayers is dependent upon our liberality to the poor" (Marion G. Romney. "The Blessings of the Fast" Ensign. July, 1982). Search verses 28-30 for evidence that the above statement is true.

According to verses 31-37, why is it important to develop the attitude of improvement and repentance while in this life?

Look up what the word "exhort" means, and then look for what Amulek exhorts people to do in verses 38-41.

Day 198, Alma 35

As you read today's chapter, look for the part that "anger" plays in the story. What part does anger play in your life? Do you get angry with the word of God and His prophets? Do you want others to also be angry at those who make you angry? Does the kindness and fellowship of others toward people you dislike increase your anger? Do you express your anger to others, seeking to find those who have similar feelings?

There are many who feel left out, cast out, and in need of refuge. Notice how the people of Ammon treated those in verse 9.

This chapter tells the story of how the war that is to come started with the anger of the Zoramites and the kindness of the people of Ammon. There have been many wars because of these two beliefs and behaviors, and there will be more. Which side, which belief, and which behavior will we be on?

Day 199, Alma 36:1-24

When have you felt the fulfillment of Alma's promise in verse 3?

Which of the following principles do you find most interesting: Those who seek to destroy the Church will only bring about their own destruction or that God still desires to reclaim those who seek the destruction of his Church?

Look for how Alma describes both the pain of sin and the joy of redemption in verses 11-24.

How does feeling both the pain of sin and the joy of redemption help change us into new people?

Day 200 Alma 36:25-37:10

Yesterday, we read about how Alma changed through the Atonement. Today, look for the difference that this change made to Alma's life in Alma 36:25-28.

What does Alma tell Helaman he "ought" to know in Alma 36:29-30?

If you were writing a letter to your family, what things would you say that they ought to know?

As you read the commandments from Alma to his son Helaman about how to treat and care for the sacred records, look for what thoughts and feelings you get about how to treat and care for the sacred records that have come to you.

Day 201, Alma 37:11-25

In verses 11-20, notice, and maybe even mark, the words "purpose," "power," and "promises."

Why was it a wise thing, on God's part, to give the world the Book of Mormon? In what ways have you seen the power of God manifested lately? What promises has God made to you that have been fulfilled?

We should not be upset that we don't understand everything yet. Even Alma didn't know the mysteries of God "fully" (:11).

Verses 16-17 are very insightful if you change the intent from caring for the plates, to caring for children.

Verses 21-25 deal with the Urim and Thummim, seer stone, and the translation of the Book of Mormon and the Jaredite plates. A couple of great articles about this are: "Joseph the Seer" by Richard Turley in the October 2015 Ensign; "Book of Mormon Translation" found in the Gospel topic essays, or under the Church History tab on the Gospel Library app; and "A New Prophet and a New Scripture: The Coming Forth of the Book of Mormon" by Kenneth W. Godfrey in the January 1988 Ensign. The Book of Mormon is truly a miraculous book with a miraculous faith-promoting story about its translation.

Day 202, Alma 37:26-42

In verses 26-34, look for what Alma instructs his son to teach, and also look for what he is not to teach. Why do you think it is important for a teacher to know that just because something is true—like how the Devil has powerful secret signs and lies—it doesn't need to receive much of our time and attention?

What bit of counsel from verses 35-37 could be applied by you to improve the quality of your day?

The Lord has always given divine gifts to help point and direct His children so that they might have many small miracles day by day (:28-42). What types of gifts do you have that work according to the same formula as the Liahona? What do these verses also say about how to limit daily miracles?

Day 203, Alma 37:43-38:8

For most of the world's history, the greatest hindrance to heeding the words of Christ were lack of availability and illiteracy. In our country, many are unable to heed the words of Christ because of spiritual apathy. There has never been a group of people in the history of the earth who have had access to the words of Christ as easily as we now do. Why does the warning in Alma 37:43-47 seem even more accurate today than it was then?

Twice in Alma 38:1-5, Alma tells his son Shiblon that he has "great joy" in him. In those same verses, look for what Alma identifies about Shiblon that allowed him to bring great joy to himself, others, and God. Which of those things will help you experience greater joy today?

Read Alma 38:6-8 and then complete the following phrase: If there is bitter pain and anguish of soul, then the solution is to _____; then you will find _____.

Day 204, Alma 38:9-39:9

Each of us has some responsibility to teach and to lead people. Shiblon, Alma's son, is already a good teacher and preacher. Now his father gives some killer advice, verse for verse, about how to become an even greater teacher and leader. As you read Alma 38:9-15, consider what you may need to do to become a greater teacher to those for whom you have responsibility.

Why do you think that bridling your passions, instead of giving into them, leads to being filled with love (38:12)?

One of the reasons that Alma may have counseled Shiblon to bridle his passions is because his little brother, Corianton, failed to do so. As you study Alma 39:1-9, consider these questions: What could have been done to prevent this situation? What do these verses teach us about the seriousness of sexual sin? Why is sexual sin serious?

Day 205, Alma 39:10-40:10

In Alma 39:10-19, Alma continues his counsel to his struggling son Corianton. What would you say are the two or three most important morsels of counsel that were delivered today? Which of today's counsel could help someone you love who struggles? How will you share or teach this counsel with those whom you love?

In Alma 40:1-10, what does Alma say about mysteries and the resurrection?

What doctrine does God want to reveal to you, but is waiting for you to diligently inquire about?

Day 206, Alma 40:11-26

In your Bible Dictionary, look up the word "hell" and discover how many ways this term can be used in LDS theology. In what ways does what you learned match up with verses 11-14?

In verses 15-26, what does Alma say and what does he not say about the resurrection?

What things are you personally looking forward to being restored through the resurrection?

Day 207, Alma 41

As you read, notice the words "restore" and "restoration." Consider what those words mean.

Alma used the word restoration to teach a particular part about the doctrine of the resurrection. How would you describe the difference between restoration and resurrection, and in what ways are they associated?

Usually, when we talk or teach about the resurrection, we tend to focus on the physicality of it, but with Alma's teaching regarding restoration, our views should be enlarged. When your body and spirit are rejoined, what attributes, both physical and otherwise, would you like to have restored?

Day 208, Alma 42:1-25

Another way to word the concern in verse 1 would be: "If God really loved his children then why would he ever punish or damn any of them?" How would you answer this question after reading Alma's response in verses 1-25?

To help with this, we are going to provide descriptions of the Laws of Justice and Mercy.

The Law of Justice: For every obedience to the law, there is a blessing, which produces joy. For every disobedience of the law, there is a punishment, which produces suffering.

The Law of Mercy: Someone else can suffer, if they are able, and if they are willing.

The Laws of Justice and Mercy work on both a macro and micro level. What role will they play in your life today?

Many people misunderstand the power of God. What does Alma 42:13, 22 and D&C 29:36 teach us about how carefully God treats laws? How is this the source of His power?

Day 209, Alma 42:26-43:14

The words "And thus" found in Alma 42:26 refer to Jesus Christ's power to bring all mankind back into God's presence through the resurrection. This power then allows them to stay in God's presence through their faith and repentance because of the Atonement. With that understanding, read Alma 42:26-31 and look for what choices we each have. How much sway does the justice, mercy, and longsuffering of God have in your life?

There is no reason to suppose that Corianton was not among those mentioned in Alma 42:1-2.

In Alma 43:4-14, look for the different reasons that the Lamanites, Amalekites, and Nephites are each willing to fight. Which of those reasons can you understand?

Day 210, Alma 43:15-26

What is the difference between the Nephite and Lamanite levels of preparedness in verses 15-21? How do you prepare yourself physically, spiritually, and emotionally each day?

President Henry B. Eyring was once struggling to get an answer from the Lord, and he asked President Harold B. Lee, almost in desperation, "How do I get revelation?" To which President Lee said, "Hal, if you want to get revelation, do your homework." (Henry B. Eyring. "Prophecy and Personal Revelation" Ensign, April 2016). How does Moroni do his homework in order to qualify for revelation in verses 22-26? What concerns do you need to study out in your mind first, so that you can then receive divine guidance?

Day 211, Alma 43:27-40

Moroni did not think it was a sin to protect their liberty, homes, and families by using "stratagem" (:30). Look for all the different strategies that Moroni used in today's section.

In what ways were you strategic about how you protected your liberty, home, and family today?

At what point do you think the men under Moroni and Lehi's command were grateful for their leaders? Do you feel the same about your parents and leaders? Will your children feel the same way about you?

You may want to take a question like this to the Lord: "What would you have me do to further protect my liberty, home, and family?"

Day 212, Alma 43:41-54

We know the reasons that we say and do things are important. In verses 41-48, you will see not only the reasons why the Nephites and Lamanites are fighting, but also what impact those reasons had on the quality of their fighting. Think of something that you do for a "better cause" (:45), or at least with the right intent. How has having the correct motive improved the quality of your performance?

In verses 46-47, what counsel did the Lord offer the Nephites about war and fighting?

Even with proper motives, the Nephites needed additional strength in the middle of a difficult task. Look in verses 49-50 for what they did to obtain the additional strength that they needed. We have covered this principle before, and it is worth covering again. It is really worth using today to improve any task that we have before us?

Day 213, Alma 44:1-15

Why do you think it is important not to desire the destruction of your enemies, even though they may force you to fight them (:1-2)?

In verses 1-7, look for the reasons that Moroni believes caused his army to win the battle. Then, read verses 8-9 and look for the reasons that Zerahemnah believed caused the Nephites to win the battle. When we talk with other people, we often see things differently than they do, because our beliefs cause us to think differently. Rather than fighting about who is right and who is wrong, we would do better to make sure that we understand how their beliefs influence their thinking. Then, we will be in a position to explain how our beliefs cause us to think differently.

What do you love about the story in verses 10-15? Now, that you know what part you love, what principle can you learn from it and then apply?

Day 214, Alma 44:16-45:14

In Alma 44:16-20, look for how the Lamanites changed their opinion about making and keeping covenants. God, like Moroni, is also willing to make covenants with people when they are ready, even though they may have already rejected the opportunity to make one.

In Alma 45:1, notice how the Nephites respond to the Savior helping them in their battle.

In Alma 45:2-8, Alma interviews his son Helaman before issuing the plates into his care. Go ahead and answer the questions and be ready to receive the promised blessing.

Alma 45:9-14 contains a prophecy of Alma. This prophecy came with the instruction not to publish or make it known until after it was fulfilled. Moroni, who abridged this prophecy, was the one who saw every part of it fulfilled.

Day 215, Alma 45:15-46:10

In Alma 45:15-17, look for what is blessed and cursed. What evidence has there been that these prophetic blessings and curses are legitimate?

We don't know anything for sure, but the verses in Alma 45:18-19 are interesting.

In Alma 45:20-46:10, look for why the people were in need of the word and why they rejected it.

Discover the three lessons that Mormon wanted us to learn from this time in Nephite history in Alma 46:8-10.

Why do you think the people couldn't tell the difference between these leaders' goals and motives?

Day 216, Alma 46:11-28

With Amalickiah threatening the freedom and religion of the Nephites, Captain Moroni takes action. Which part of this story is your favorite: Captain Moroni's preparation in verses 11-15, Moroni's prayer for his people and country in verses 16-18, Moroni's presentation to the people in 19-20, the people's reaction to Moroni in 21-22, or Moroni's interpretation of Father Jacob's prophecy in verses 23-28?

Do you think Moroni rent his coat because of Jacob's prophecy?

Moroni listed the things that he was willing to defend and fight for. What are the things that you are willing to defend and fight for?

In your life right now, is there a Moroni for you follow, or do you need to become Moroni?

Day 217, Alma 46:29-41

Notice the difference that being confident in their cause made for the leaders and followers of both groups in verses 29-35.

In what way are each of us also given the choice between covenant and death?

In verse 36, Captain Moroni hoisted the title of liberty on every tower and also planted it among the people. What types of principles and truths have you hoisted for your family, and which ones have you been able to plant?

In verses 39-41, look for how they were blessed in death and sickness. What types of things would you add to update these verses?

Day 218, Alma 47:1-19

In verses 1-8, we learn more about Amalickiah's desires and goals. Notice who he cares about and who he does not care about.

Look for what strategies Amalickiah used to get what he desired. In what ways are these same strategies implemented by Satan to trick and displace people in our day? How does he get people to feel safe enough to come down from where they are protected? Why is it better for him to poison by degrees rather than in one lethal dose?

Day 219, Alma 47:20-36

Notice how Amalickiah used a custom of the Nephites and Lamanites to kill the king of the Lamanites in verses 20-24. Customs and traditions of both culture and family can be a hindrance to discipleship. Look for how carefully Elder Richard G. Scott introduced this same idea in a General Conference talk. "Because of the sensitive nature of what I want to say, and to not be misunderstood, please consider that you and I are alone in a quiet place. Imagine that we have deep bonds of friendship and a relationship of trust that permits open communication. Let us assume that you have asked me how to benefit most from your membership in The Church of Jesus Christ of Latter-day Saints. I know you to be a person of faith and conviction. I also know you intensely value your unique cultural heritage. There are threads of that heritage woven into the very fiber of your being. You have obtained great benefit from it and you desire to be a root sunk deeply into the soil of that heritage so that your children and grandchildren will benefit as well. Yet I see how some elements of that pattern of life can conflict with the teachings of Jesus Christ and could bring disappointment or difficulty. As a friend, I want to help you see this potential without offending you or in any way lessening those precious portions of your heritage that should be preserved and built upon." ("Removing Barriers to Happiness" Ensign, May. 1998). This whole talk is remarkable and worth a read. What traditions and culture do you have that may be blocking blessings of happiness from coming to you?

In the rest of today's verses, we will see how Amalickiah and his servants gain control over the Lamanite kingdom through fraud and cunning. They gained a kingdom, but at what cost? There is a good chance that today you will be placed in a situation where lying will be a temptation. I invite you to be honest and not gain a good score, money, approval from others, or even a kingdom if it means you must lie.

There is a very interesting idea presented in verse 36. This idea is explained by Joseph Smith who was telling about the troubles caused by apostate members. "When the Prophet had ended telling how he had been treated, Brother Behunin remarked: 'If I should leave this Church I would not do as those men have done: I would go to some remote place where Mormonism had never been heard of, settle down, and no one would ever learn that I knew anything about it.' The great Seer immediately replied: 'Brother Behunin, you don't know what you would do. No doubt these men once thought as you do. Before you joined this Church you stood on neutral ground. When the gospel was preached, good and evil were set before you. You could choose either or neither. There were two opposite masters inviting you to serve them. When you joined this Church you enlisted to serve God. When you did that you left the neutral ground, and you never can get back on to it. Should you forsake the Master you enlisted to serve, it will be by the instigation of the evil one, and you will follow his dictation and be his servant.'" (Teachings of The Presidents of The Church: Joseph Smith, p.324).

Day 220, Alma 48:1-18

Captain Moroni put a Title of Liberty on every tower to remind the Nephites that they were fighting for family, liberty, and God (Alma 46:36). In verses 1-6, what did Amalickiah put on top of the Lamanite towers? What was his purpose in doing this?

In verse 17, we learn that if all men and women would be like Captain Moroni, then the powers of hell would have been shaken forever. Look for what made him a hell-shaker in verses 7-18. Which of those will you do really well today?

Read verse 18 and discover who else possessed these same qualities that Moroni had. Then, read Mosiah 28:4 to see what used to be said about them. What does that teach you about the power of the Atonement? For whom would you like to see a similar change? By what power do you believe that it could happen?

Day 221, Alma 48:19-49:8

I like the phrase, "no less serviceable unto the people" in Alma 48:19. Your service, though most of it will be unnoticed, is no less important that other leaders or members.

In Alma 48:21-25, look for words that describe the Nephites' attitudes toward war and conflict. In what ways can a marriage, family, and friendship be blessed if we have similar attitudes about conflict in those relationships?

What lessons could a person with a troubled or shaky past learn from the cities of the Nephites in Alma 49:1-8?

Day 222, Alma 49:9-24

What did Captain Moroni do to take care of those who were once weak and vulnerable in verses 9-17?

In verses 18-24, look for how important the entrance was in this battle. What can this story teach us about how careful we should be with what we allow to enter our homes and our minds?

Day 223, Alma 49:25-50:12

Notice the responses in Alma 49:26-28. Which way will you respond to the situations that you will face today?

Look for what additional preparations Moroni makes to each city (Alma 50:1-12). Moroni had been successful in many battles. Why do you think it is important that he continued to add additional protections? What are you doing now to grow and develop yourself and family that you were not doing a few years ago?

A friend of mine related an experience he had attending elders quorum meetings. He noticed that the men rarely shared current spiritual experiences, but instead often talked about events of their missions and things they learned then. My friend was saddened to think that these good men hadn't been "increasing daily" in their spirituality (:12). Fruit only grows on new wood. Like Moroni, we must work daily to grow and further prepare ourselves.

Day 224, Alma 50:13-34

In verse 23, it is recorded that following the failed attacks of the Lamanites upon the fortified cities, the Nephites experienced a period of tremendous happiness. Look for how they were blessed in verses 13-24. Verses 19, and 21 teach us that these blessings are a result of God's words being "verified." When have you felt that God's promised blessings have been verified in your life recently?

This great Nephite peace is threatened because of a "warm contention" that developed between the Nephite people (:26). You may have felt the beginnings of a "warm contention" coming on in your own life. Why is it important that we cool these feelings before they spark into flames of rage?

Morianton's rebellion and contention could have caused great difficulty for the Nephites if it had not been for the courage of a maid servant (:26-34). This maid was the victim of physical abuse. Morianton is described as "a man of much passion" (:30). This is a common excuse by those who commit such crimes and abuses—that they can't control their passions. This young woman didn't blame herself, she survived, she fled the situation, she went and found a person/parent/leader that she could trust, and she told them everything that happened. Not only did she save the Nephite people, but she set an wonderful example about how to respond to abuse.

Day 225, Alma 50:35-51:12

As you read today's section, look for all of the different enemies the Nephites faced. Do you ever feel like you have one trial, enemy, or hardship right after another? Consider what would have happened if there had not been a Teancum, Helaman, Pahoran, and the voice of the people. God always sends leaders fit for the enemy of the time. What enemies of the kingdom were you born to fight?

What do you like about how the Nephites treated the people of Morianton when they returned in Alma 50:35-36?

In Alma 51:8, we learn why the king-men desired leadership. How would you complete the following statement: A true leader should desire . . .

Day 226, Alma 51:13-21

Sometimes there's confusion about Moroni's actions in today's section, but it is important to remember what the king-men were threatening (:13, 16). Then, look at what resulted from Moroni's actions in verses 17-21.

Have you ever had the same feelings and ideas as Captain Moroni in verse 14?

Why do you think the idea of nobility can be dangerous (:17-18, and 21)?

Day 227, Alma 51:22-37

Look for what resulted from the Nephite infighting in verses 22-25. In what ways does that same type of destruction happen to our wards and families when we also have infighting?

Personally, I find verses 26-27 terrifying. We have no explanation for why these great and strong cities fell, only the fact that one weaker city fell and then many other great cities fell.

Pro Football Hall of Fame receiver Jerry Rice, when describing his intense summer workout regimen, frequently says, "Today I will do what others won't, so tomorrow I can accomplish what others can't." As you read verses 29-37, look for examples of how this same principle is used by Teancum and his men. What will you do today, so that tomorrow you can do what God needs you to do?

Day 228, Alma 52:1-18

For today, I want you to consider what principles can be learned from each of these phrases:

- "Ready to give them battle on that day" (:1).
- "For they had not taken any cities save they had lost much blood" (:4).
- "Truly he was preparing to defend himself against them"(:6).
- "Seek every opportunity to scourge the Lamanites in that quarter" (:10).

- "That perhaps he might take again by stratagem" (:10).
- "And thus he was endeavoring to harass the Nephites, and to draw away a part of their forces" (:13).
- "And thus were the Nephites in those dangerous circumstances" (:14).
- "He saw that it was impossible that he could overpower them while they were in their fortifications" (:17).
- "To wait for the coming of . . . that he might receive strength to his army" (:17).

Day 229, Alma 52:19-40

We are accustomed to thinking of Moroni as good, and he is, but he is also a great war strategist. The Lamanites were safe as long as they stayed in their fortified cities, their strongholds. Only by deceiving or decoying the Lamanites out of their fortified strongholds could Moroni have a chance to defeat them and retake the city. Satan uses this same tactic on us today. What, who, and where are your strongholds? How does Satan try to decoy you into believing it is ok for you to leave these fortified places?

Why is it so impressive that a man of war, a man who spends his time thinking about victory, earning his pay and livelihood through battle, also seeks for opportunities to end battles and bloodshed as soon as his opponents allow (:32-40)? If a man of battle and war could also be a man seeking for peace, then can't we all avoid a few more arguments in our lives?

Day 230, Alma 53:1-9

As you read verses 1-5, look for the reason why Moroni kept the Lamanite prisoners busy. Who else benefits from labor and work?

While Moroni had gained a major victory (:6-7), the Lamanites were also successful because of iniquity, dissension, and intrigue among the Nephites (:8-9). How might these same things be costing us the victory of battles in our own homes?

Day 231, Alma 53:10-23

Look for how oaths and covenants affected the lives of the people in today's section.

What kinds of things led to these people being so loyal to their oaths and covenants?

What are your feelings about the covenants that you have made? Do you remember them? Could you name them?

When was the last time that you made a choice or took an action because of your covenants?

Day 232, Alma 54

During the battles there have been several prisoners taken on both sides. Alma 54 contains letters addressing a possible exchange of prisoners between Moroni and Ammoron. Look at how bold Moroni was in his faith and belief in verses 5-14.

Then look at how bold Ammoron was in his doubt and unbelief in verses 15-24.

As I read this, I couldn't help thinking about Michael Otterson's quote about defending the faith. He said, "There are words I prefer to use other than 'defend.' If all we ever play is a defensive game, the most we can hope for is a draw. While it can be extraordinarily difficult when under attack or critique from unfriendly voices, it's important that we try not to sound defensive. We would do better to explain or promote an idea, concept or principle. For example, when *"The Book of Mormon"* musical first surfaced, despite its blasphemy, crudeness and bad language, we opted for a non-defensive statement that taught a principle. Our much-quoted response was: *"The Book of Mormon"* musical may attempt to entertain audiences for an evening, but the Book of Mormon as a volume of scripture will change people's lives forever by bringing them closer to Christ.' As many of you know, we even took out ads in the show's Playbill, inviting people who had seen the show to now 'Read the Book.'" (Michael R. Otterson. "On The Record" 2015 FairMormon Conference).

What will you do to be bold at promoting the gospel and not just defending it in the coming weeks?

Day 233, Alma 55:1-27

Moroni and his spy defeated this group of Lamanite guards because they could not guard their desires (:12). In what ways has this tactic worked on you in the past? How will being more mindful of this tactic help you in the future?

What does this story teach us about those who would pretend to be our friends?

It was important to arm those who were prisoners (:16-20). What amount of confidence do you think that gave to those prisoners? How do we arm those who are in spiritual prisons so that they can also feel hope and encouragement?

Look for how a couple of simple principles in verse 19 helped to guide the actions of Captain Moroni.

Day 234, Alma 55:28-56:17

There are often times where we find ourselves in situations that we or others have been in before. When this happens, we might simply do what was done before without trying to really analyze, ponder, or seek revelation. Look for how the Lamanites fall victim to this in Alma 55:28-35.

How can a person not love the logic of Alma 55:32? How might someone rewrite this verse to become a modern day warning of something we face?

In Alma 56:1-17, look for how the belief and commitment of the 2,000 sons of Helaman impacted those around them. What impact will your righteousness have on others today?

Day 235, Alma 56:18-38

Being mindful of one's weakness and what makes one weak can protect us (:18-26). What are some of the weak spots where you need to be careful?

In these same verses, notice how hard the enemy fought to maintain what they took. Satan does not yield ground easily; it often takes time and planning to recover what he takes, like in verses 27-37. We cannot go to places where Satan is strong to win back those who have been taken; they must be lured out of his strongholds. What or who do you want to retake from the adversary? How might you persuade them to follow you? Helaman used Antipus, who else can help you in your recovery efforts?

One of the major reasons that the Lamanites chased Helaman's army was because they were "increasing daily" in their forces and strength (:29). A fortress, if not maintained, will soon be insufficient for the battles to come. As we seek for daily increase from the Lord, we will find that our strength will always be sufficient for the day.

Day 236, Alma 56:39-57

"We were not sufficiently strong to contend with them" (:39). There are times when we will find ourselves in situations where we will feel pursued to exhaustion. What can the Sons of Helaman teach us in verses 39-42?

Often we must face situations we don't want to experience, similar to how Helaman and his sons felt about battle. Look for the reasons they were willing to take on this unwelcomed task in verses 43-48. Which of those reasons listed will give you strength and courage to take on your unwelcomed task?

How has the miracle mentioned in verses 49-57 helped you throughout your life?

Day 237, Alma 57:1-16

Verses 1-4 are a good reminder that the enemy of our souls is a liar who bluffs of his strength and position.

What ideas and revelation can you get about how to bring people back to the faith through Helaman's example of reclaiming a city in verses 6-12?

Look at how caring about their prisoners placed greater hardship on the Nephites (:13-16). Why is it important that we care about prisoners and those who add difficulty to our lives?

Day 238, Alma 57:17-36

The guards who took the Lamanite prisoners said, "they returned in a season to save us" (:17). The timing of many things is so precise that it becomes a witness of God's hand. This story is found in verses 28-35. What is your most recent story about the precise timing of God?

The miracle of the 2,060 sons of Helaman being saved is incredible. Look for everything that they did that assisted this miracle in verses 19-27.

What lesson are we to learn from the fact that all of the sons survived, but all were wounded to some degree (:25)?

Day 239, Alma 58:1-12

How great would verse 1 be if it was describing our responses to Satan's temptations?

There are times when you will feel weak and vulnerable, while it may appear that the enemy is getting stronger. When this happens, we, like the Nephites, can "wait" (:3-9), or we can "pour out our souls in prayer to God, that he would strengthen and deliver us" (:10). Look for what the result of the soul pouring prayer is in verses 11-12. These two verses really do contain powerful promises.

Pour out your soul in prayer and watch for the fulfillment of these same promises in your own life come to pass.

Day 240, Alma 58:13-29

I love the phrase in verse 15, "when they saw that we were not strong according to our numbers." There are times when I catch a reflection of myself in a window or a mirror and I think, "That is not a very good representation of what you really are." We can be so much more than what others might perceive us to be when we have really prayed for strength from God (:10-12).

How many different times have we seen the Lamanites tricked into leaving their fortifications (:16-18)? If we leave people, places, practices, and principles that protect and strengthen us, we will be placed in dangerous circumstances.

The strategy the Nephites used to win the city in verses 16-29 was the result of their prayer for strength and help. God, through the Holy Ghost, will provide inspired thoughts and feelings that, if acted upon, will bless our lives and others. What thoughts and feelings has God sent recently to strengthen and protect you?

Because of a little extra discomfort, work, and strain, in one night the Nephites were able to take back the city of Manti (:25-29). With the beginning of school, my wife selects a theme to help motivate us to work, toil, and try a little harder. This year the theme is "Be Excellent." We have tied it to a quote from President Hinckley, which says, "This is the great day of decision for each of us. For many it is the time of beginning something that will go on for as long as you live. I plead with you: don't be a scrub! Rise to the high ground of spiritual, mental, and physical excellence. You can do it. You may not be a genius. You may be lacking in some skills. But so many of us can do better than we are now doing. We are members of this great Church whose influence is now felt over the world. We are people with a present and with a future. Don't muff your opportunities. Be excellent." ("Our Quest for Excellence" Ensign, Sep 2010).

Helaman and his sons knew this principle. In what ways and forms will you be excellent today?

Day 241, Alma 58:30-59:13

In Alma 58:30-41, Helaman closes his letter to Moroni, which started in chapter 56. These final few verses and summary are loaded with faith, insight, and humility. Which is your favorite?

In Alma 59, look for what caused Moroni to have great rejoicing and exceeding anger.

How well does the teaching in Alma 59:9 work if you replace the word "city" with the word "people?" Who do you think is a person you can assist in maintaining their faith so that they won't have to be reclaimed one day?

Day 242, Alma 60:1-13

In this chapter, Captain Moroni begins a letter written to his government leaders. It is a criticism and condemnation of their neglect and lack of action. Moroni is missing critical information regarding the circumstances behind the apparent neglect. That is our first lesson. Nearly any time I want to be critical of someone and condemn their action, or lack thereof, there is important information that I do not possess.

Despite the fact that Moroni wrote this letter based on false premises, there are still principles of truth contained in it. You may want to mark the word "neglect" in verses 5-6 and 9-10. The Holy Ghost, unlike Moroni, is in possession of all the facts (D&C 35:19). If you were neglecting something that was very important, the Holy Ghost would reveal it if you were sincerely seeking Heaven's correction.

Look for the false assumptions that Moroni corrects in verses 11-13. In what ways do you see these false assumptions in modern sayings or beliefs in our day?

Day 243, Alma 60:14-28

In verses 14-17, Moroni lays out what led to the Nephites' current predicament. As you read, you will notice that these same reasons also lead many families, wards, and communities into predicaments.

There are so many in need that find themselves in similar circumstances as Moroni, Helaman, and their armies. I couldn't help but feel that Moroni's words in verses 18-23 are timely once more. What thoughts and feelings did you have as you read these verses?

What do you love about Moroni's courage and passion in verses 24-28?

Day 244, Alma 60:29-61:5

Do you think the warning in Alma 60:29 is as true for us as it was for them?

Who or what is impeding your progress (60:30)?

In Alma 60:32, Moroni corrects another false assumption.

What does Alma 60:34-36 say about what does and does not matter to Moroni? How do you feel about those same things?

In chapter 61, Pahoran responds to Moroni's letter. He begins to set the record straight by declaring who finds joy in Moroni's circumstance and who does not. Where a person finds joy and sorrow can reveal much about us. What will your joy and sorrow prove about you today?

Day 245, Alma 61:6-21

In verses 6-8, Pahoran updates Moroni on the government takeover.

Every line in verses 9-14 denotes the greatness of Pahoran. Pay attention to words such as "if," "but," "resist," and "therefore." How great would it be if everyone avoided taking offense as well as Pahoran did?

Back in Alma 60:33, Moroni received a revelation from the Lord that appeared wrong and misguided until you read Alma 61:19-20. Moroni and Pahoran were both lacking something. What we have here is a great example of "revelation being scattered among us" as President Boyd. K. Packer said (Quoted by Elder Neal L. Anderson. "Align with the Brethren" The Leadership Enrichment Series. August 15, 2012). This is one reason why counseling with councils is so important. When have you experienced revelation being scattered among us?

Day 246, Alma 62:1-18

How well do verses 1-2 describe so much of our lives? There is almost always someone or something to bring us "exceedingly great joy," and there is almost always something or someone that causes us to "mourn exceedingly."

After reading verses 3-11, come up with a principle or truth that you learned based on each of the following ideas: standards, gatherings, law, country, and freedom.

Why would it have been a wise and helpful thing to send a newly covenanted group of Lamanites to the people of Ammon (:15-17)?

Day 247, Alma 62:19-33

The Lamanites thought their homes were safe and protected, but they failed to remain vigilant (:19-26). What measures are you taking to remain vigilant with you home and family?

In verses 19-26, look for all the new things Moroni does to be victorious that he hasn't done before. Each of these little variants demonstrates superb leadership. What quality demonstrated by Moroni could benefit you at work, church, or at home?

What was so great about the prison system of the Nephites in verses 27-30? What similarities do think these verses have with spirit prison and work for the dead?

Day 248, Alma 62:34-52

Today in verses 34-38, we will say goodbye to Ammoron, Teancum, and the war. Consider the impact produced by the death of these two leaders. What will end in the world with your death? What types of things continue because your life does?

For sixteen years the Nephites have been at war with the Lamanites and various defectors. In verse 41, we learn that many became hardened and many became softened. Your life and trials may be long and challenging, but each of us gets to decide if we will become hardened or softened. What will be your reaction to challenging situations and people today?

In verses 45-52, Helaman and his brethren preach the gospel with great success. Sixteen years earlier they tried the same thing, only to receive rejection (Alma 45:22-24). Look for how sixteen years of diligence and prayers made the difference in helping people receiving the message this time.

Day 249, Alma 63

Verses 4-10 contain an interesting story about the Nephite explorer Hagoth. Both tradition and prophets have said some of the inhabitants of the Pacific islands are descendants from these voyages.

To the Saints in New Zealand, President Joseph F. Smith said, "You brothers and sisters from New Zealand, I want you to know that you are from the people of Hagoth" (quoted by Spencer W. Kimball in Joseph Fielding McConkie and Robert L. Millet, Doctrinal Commentary on the Book of Mormon, vol. 3 [1991], 329).

In the dedicatory prayer for the Hamilton New Zealand Temple, President David O. McKay said, "We express gratitude that to these fertile Islands Thou didst guide descendants of Father Lehi, and hast enabled them to prosper" ("Dedicatory Prayer Delivered by Pres. McKay at New Zealand Temple," Church News, May 10, 1958, 2).

President Spencer W. Kimball said: "It is reasonable to conclude that Hagoth and his associates were about nineteen centuries on the islands, from about 55 B.C. to 1854, before the gospel began to reach them. They had lost all the plain and precious things which the Savior brought to the earth, for they were likely on the islands when the Christ was born in Jerusalem" (Temple View Area Conference Report, February 1976, 3; quoted in Joseph Fielding McConkie and Robert L. Millet, Doctrinal Commentary on the Book of Mormon, vol. [1991] 3, 329).

This chapter also traces the passing of the sacred records from Helaman to Shiblon to Helaman's son Helaman (Alma 63:1-3, and 11-13).

We have just completed the largest book, 63 chapters, 161 pages, and only 39 years. If you subtract a few concentrated days of the Savior's ministry in 3 Nephi, the time in Alma gets the most coverage. Why do you think the writers spent so many pages on this time period?

Day 250, Helaman 1:1-17

Look for all of the people who are seeking power in today's section and the reasons they do so. What problems can improper motives cause in our lives?

What lesson do you think we are learn from the fact that Kishkumen, who made a covenant that no one would know what he did, was mentioned by name several times (:9-12)?

Day 251, Helaman 1:18-34

Do you think that contention in our lives and families produces the same consequences that it did for the Nephite government (:18)?

In the midst of war strategies, we get a great verse about the importance of gathering. What lesson can we learn about gathering from verse 24?

In verses 25-34, we learn about a tactical error that Coriantumr made, which resulted in being surrounded by his enemy. In what ways might people today make decisions that result in circumstances where they also feel surrounded?

Day 252, Helaman 2

Kishkumen is back, and his goal is to do dark things in dark places that no one will know about (:3-4). His name is mentioned even more times in this chapter than the last. For those who are unrepentant, the promised publication of their wickedness is the same, according to D&C 1:2-3.

What do you think is so dangerous and enslaving about trying to keep dark deeds a secret that Mormon would warn us that this idea almost led the Nephites to their destruction (:13-14)?

Who do you know whose destruction was, or almost was, brought about by trying to keep dark deeds a secret? If there are any secret dark deeds in your life, I invite you to let the Lord shine His healing light upon them. The message of the Book of Mormon is clear: Secret dark deeds lead to destruction. Only faith in Christ, repentance, and the Atonement bring salvation.

Day 253, Helaman 3:1-18

One of the blessings and challenges of being a member of a church is that you interact frequently with other people. This interacting can help us develop Christlike character in extraordinary ways, but it can also cause some bumps, bruises, and contention. Notice what kinds of contention the Nephites were having in verses 1-3. What can you do to make sure your little contentions and dissensions diminish rather than increase?

In verses 4-18, Mormon gives us a brief summary of the travels, building, and shipping ventures of those who left Zarahemla. Mormon then points out in verse 14 that not even a hundredth part of their record can be included. Does that figure create a longing for more of the record or a desire to cherish what we have been given?

Day 254, Helaman 3:19-37

In verses 19-26, see what you can learn about Helaman, the Church, and the Gadiantons during this time.

Brace yourself for more astounding "thus we see" and "we see" statements from Mormon in verses 27, 28, and 29-30. Each one of these contains vitally important promises. Which one are you most attracted to at this time? What did these scriptures say we must do to inherit these promises?

Verses 31-37 reveal some causes of pride and some of the blessings of humility. These verses cover a lot of years, and these years are known for either pride or humility. What will you do today that will help you to have a year of humility?

Day 255, Helaman 4:1-17

Look for what contention and dissension cost the Nephites in verses 1-8. What are some things that contention and dissension have cost you?

In verses 9-10, we have the story of the Nephites regaining half of what they lost. Why is it important to know that we can regain that which was once lost?

In verses 11-13, we learn about what led to the contention and dissension in the first place. Was there anything in this list that surprised you? Then, in verses 14-17, we see what created the conditions so that which was lost could be found. How does verse 15 show us the ways in which repentance can help us? Which of these two processes do you feel you need to be aware of and why?

Day 256, Helaman 4:18-5:4

Yesterday, we saw that the Nephites lost part of their lands to the Lamanites in war. They were then able to regain half of what they lost. Finally, the Nephites reached a point where they could regain no more of their land (4:18-19). While it is true that we can be forgiven of our sins and mistakes, the potential happiness that we could have had is lost.

Sin and wickedness always brings loss. Look for what the Nephites lost because of their wickedness in Helaman 4:20-26. Wickedness leads to what kind of weakness?

Do you think Nephi is fighting or giving up in Helaman 5:1-4?

Day 257, Helaman 5:5-13

Many of the words that we will read today are from the counsel Helaman spoke to his sons Nephi and Lehi. As you read verses 5-13, search for what a father desired of his sons and also what he wanted them to remember.

116

Of those points, which do you think will make a difference if you remember it today?

If you are a parent, what are the things you desire for your children and what do you want them to remember?

What do you think your earthly and Heavenly Parents desire for you and what do they want you to remember?

How many times have you experienced the promises of verse 12 in your life? What would happen if people forgot these great teachings about Christ?

Day 258, Helaman 5:14-52

Look for the difference it made when these brothers remembered their father's teachings about Christ and then shared those teachings with others in verses 14-19.

The rest of chapter 5 deals with the imprisonment of Nephi and Lehi and their miraculous deliverance. Look for how the same event was experienced by each of the following: Nephi and Lehi (:20-26), the Lamanites and Nephite dissenters (:27-34), Aminadab (:35-41), and the whole group (:42-52).

In what ways were each shown the power of God?

When was a time that you experienced the power of God in such a way that it changed you?

Day 259, Helaman 6:1-14

From the years 62-65 of the reign of the judges, the Nephites and Lamanites experienced an incredible time. As you read verses 1-14, look for what made is time so unique.

Are you frequently experiencing the feelings and relationships that the members of the church did in verse 3? What do you think would need to happen so that you and others could experience that more often?

Day 260, Helaman 6:15-30

Look for how the Lamanites, and then the Nephites, reacted to the discovery of Gadianton's robbers and murderers being among them (:20-21). How do you think your country, community, or family would react?

What is the difference between the covenants of the temple and the secret oaths and covenants of Gadianton's robbers and murderers in verses 22-24? What kinds of activities do your temple covenants motivate you to do?

These secret oaths were so dangerous that Alma commanded his son to make sure they did not go forth to the world (:25, and 25a). We are informed in verses 26-30 that these oaths were again being brought forth by Satan. You may want to mark the phrase "that same being" in these verses. If you were to write your own verse describing the activities "that same being" has been up to lately, what would be included?

Day 261, Helaman 6:31-41

In this critical moment for the Nephites and the Lamanites, look for what each group did to grow in righteousness or wickedness. Each day we are presented with opportunities to grow in righteousness and wickedness.

What will you trample under your feet today: commandments or temptations?

Will the spirit be poured out upon you or withdrawn?

What will you build up, and what will you hunt down?

Day 262, Helaman 7:1-12

In verses 1-6, we get a description of Nephi's mission to the north country and his reflection about the government in his own land.

Have you ever wished for something similar to Nephi from his prayer in verses 7-9?

Have your recent prayers been quick status updates or have they been soul pouring?

Day 263, Helaman 7:13-8:10

Yesterday, Nephi climbed his tower and poured his soul out to God. In Helaman 7:13-15, you will discover why he was on his tower. What are the things and who are the people that cause you to climb towers/temples to mourn and pray?

In Helaman 7:16-29, discover what the Nephites and Lamanites gained and what they lost because of their choices. What gains do you get from wickedness that is worth the loss?

Search for the reasons that people give to not believe and also to believe in prophets in Helaman 8:1-10.

Day 264, Helaman 8:11-28

In verses 11-13, Nephi speaks of God giving power to his prophets. What has convinced you that God really has given power to prophets today?

Moses lifted up a brass serpent upon a pole to heal ancient Israel when they were bitten by venomous serpents. Nephi declares that there is a key lesson that we are to learn from this in verse 15. Why do you think this simple gesture of looking with faith can be so incredibly humiliating and hard sometimes?

In verse 24, Nephi proclaims that the people have rejected the abundant evidence about Christ and His prophets. Look for what evidence was cited in verses 13-23. What are a couple of updates you would make to this list?

Day 265, Helaman 9:1-18

Today, we will see how five men became convinced that Nephi was a true prophet.

What are the circumstances that caused you to believe that God has placed real prophets upon the earth today?

What difference does it make when you really believe that God has put prophets among us?

Day 266, Helaman 9:19-41

Yesterday, we saw the testimony of prophets grow in five men. Today, Nephi will make even more specific, detailed prophecies. Look for what effect the combined force of these six testimonies have on the people?.

What were the reasons the crowd of people gave for not believing in Nephi, and what were the reasons that Nephi offered in verses 19-24? What do you think modern prophets and doubters might add to each list?

What can this section of scripture teach us about the gifts and accuracy of prophets, seers, and revelators?

Day 267, Helaman 10:1-19

Nephi is going to have a remarkable experience with the Lord today. What happened in verses 1-3 that prepared him for this experience? How can we better prepare for revelation by doing the same things?

In verses 4-11, look for the promises and powers that the Lord gave to Nephi. Also, look for the reasons why the Lord gave Nephi such power and promises.

From what you have learned, what do you need to do to receive greater power and promises from the Lord?

When we do what the Lord has asked us to do with exactness, and He can completely trust us, then we can work mighty miracles in His name. Nephi does several miraculous things in verses 12-19. Which of these miraculous things impressed or inspired you?

Day 268, Helaman 11:1-20

Yesterday, the Lord gave tremendous power to Nephi. Today, look for how Nephi used this sealing to bless the lives of many people. What does today's story teach you about prophets and God?

Nephi offered two different prayers in verses 3-4 and 10-16. Which prayer do you think our actions might cause a prophet to pray? Which prayer best represents your prayers on the behalf of your own loved ones?

Day 269, Helaman 11:21-38

Today's section will cover ten years of good and bad times. During the times of peace, there were a "few contentions concerning the points of doctrine laid down by the prophets" (:22). By the next verse, these few contentions have grown into "much strife" (:23). We live in a time when many are facing similar feelings. Look for what ended these feelings according to verse 23. Why do you think the words "many" and "daily" are important (:23)?

I testify that the solution to the contention and the strife has not changed and that daily immersion into the many revelations will put an end to the strife.

In verses 24-38, we will again see the "great havoc" and "great destruction" caused by dissension (:27). This system, which was created to cause fear, became established "in the space of not many years" (:32, and 26). Why is it terrifying that such great changes can come upon a whole group of people in so short a time? Why does that knowledge make the daily decisions even more important?

Day 270, Helaman 12:1-17

In verses 1-3 we get several "thus we see" statements regarding truths that Mormon wants us to learn. When have you seen examples of these truths in your own lives or in the lives of others?

In verses 4-7, we are shown how the children of God can sometimes be quick, slow, vain, and foolish. Then, in verses 8-17, we are told of the greatness of God and His power, and yet He is ignored by many of His children.

Because you do believe that God is "great [in] goodness and mercy toward" you (:6), what things will you be quick to do today, and what things will you be slow to do?

Day 271, Helaman 12:18-13:4

Today, we will continue to look at God's power. In Helaman 12:18-26, we see evidence of God's power and willingness to hide, curse, cut off, and even damn things and people. Mormon writes that he "would that all men might be saved" (:25). The only reason that people will not all be saved is because not all of them will repent (:22-24). "The Greek word of which this is the translation denotes a change of mind, a fresh view about God, about oneself, and about the world. Since we are born into conditions of mortality, repentance comes to mean a turning of the heart and will to God, and a renunciation of sin to which we are naturally inclined. Without this there can be no progress in the things of the soul's salvation, for all accountable persons are stained by sin and must be cleansed in order to enter the kingdom of heaven" (Bible Dictionary: Repentance). Repentance is us changing our thoughts, feelings, and actions in order to match the thoughts, feelings, and actions of Heavenly Father and Jesus Christ. What action, thought, or feeling does God want you to change in order to bless you with more happiness?

In Helaman 13:1-4, Samuel the Lamanite begins his ministry to the Nephites. The Lord promised Samuel that he would prophesy unto the people if he spoke the words that the Lord put into his heart. As we continue reading about Samuel's teachings, watch for how many awesome prophecies he makes about the life, death, and ministry of Jesus Christ. What kind of preparation do you think people have to make so they can also have the Lord put words into their hearts when they speak? When was the last time you heard someone speaking words that you are sure were put into his or her heart by the Lord?

Day 272, Helaman 13:5-20

Verses 5-11 contain a prophecy that is dependent upon repentance. Why do you think people get confused about repentance and stop viewing it as a blessing? Might there be blessings that you are missing out on because of something that needs repentance in your life?

Verses 12-20 declare several things about both the righteous and the wicked. From the context of the previous verses, I think it is safe to say that to be considered righteous, one must be repentant.

I have to admit that whenever I lose my keys, wallet, or cell phone, I often think of verses 18-20.

Day 273, Helaman 13:21-39

The Nephites have become so hardened to the Lord and His prophets that the only way to get through to them is by cursing them and their belongings. In verses 21-31, look for the reasons God was willing to curse this people. When you identify those qualities, you can also discover activities and attitudes that will lead to great blessings by doing or being the opposite. Which of these actions or attitudes will bless you today?

How will you be sure to reverse the actions and attitudes toward the prophets, mentioned in verses 24-26, during the next General Conference weekend?

Just as people can make their calling and election sure by continually using the Atonement, people can also have their "destruction made sure" (:32, 38). To learn how people can make their "destruction made sure," read verses 32-39, and then do the opposite to discover how to continue on the path that will lead to you making your calling and election sure.

What simple things does God want you to do today to continue on the path toward your exaltation? What simple things does God want you not to do so that you avoid the path to destruction?

Day 274, Helaman 14:1-19

What is so remarkable about verse 1?

In verses 2-8, we have Samuel prophesying about the birth of Jesus Christ. Look for what the sign of Christ's birth would be, and also look for what impact the birth of Christ will have on others.

In verses 9-13, Samuel reveals his intent for climbing upon the city wall. To whom has the Lord asked you to be a Samuel?

Because of Jesus Christ's death and resurrection, there are tremendous opportunities awarded to each of us. What are some of these opportunities mentioned in verses 14-19?

Day 275, Helaman 14:20-31

In verses 20-27, Samuel prophesies about many signs that will accompany the death of Jesus Christ. These signs would have been miraculous to have witnessed. How well do you think they fulfilled the intent for why they were given (:28-29)? These macro signs were meant for a large group of people. What micro signs have manifested in your life to help you believe that Jesus is the Christ?

Throughout the history of the world, the choices haven't changed much. That is why the content of verses 30-31 is still very relevant today. Look for what is "given" or "permitted" by God in these verses. How will you use the gifts that God has given you to become what He wants you to be today?

If you do what God wants you to do today, how will those things be "restored" unto you tomorrow (:31)?

Day 276, Helaman 15

The phrase "except ye/they repent" comes up several times in today's chapter. Look for what Samuel says will happen if they don't repent in verses 1-3 and 14-17. What would happen to the quality of your life if you stopped repenting?

Verse 3 says that the Lord chastened or corrected the Nephites because he loved them. How is correction and chastisement a sign of love? How does a person correct because of love and with love, rather than out of anger and annoyance?

Look for the blessings and benefits that repentance brought to many of the Lamanites in verses 4-14. Sin often offers only short-term pleasures, while repentance brings forth generational blessings. What is something for which could repent that would result in the blessing of your children and grandchildren?

Discover the process that happens to people when they begin to study the scriptures and the words of the prophets according to verse 7.

Day 277, Helaman 16

This whole chapter is about belief and unbelief. Look in verses 1-11 for the different actions that are taken, with respect to Samuel's talk, by those who believe and those who do not believe. Today you will act and not act based upon your belief or your unbelief. In verse 10, we are told that those who believed walked "more circumspectly before God." Circumspectly means careful and cautiously. What is the difference between doing this because one has to versus wanting to?

In verses 12-25, there are several signs and miraculous events that happen among the people. Look for all of the reasons that many people gave to convince themselves and others that the signs, prophecies, and prophets were unbelievable. How similar do you think these arguments sound to the reasons people give today for not believing in signs, prophecies, and prophets?

With all of the reasons that the world, people, and philosophies give us to not believe, why do you think Samuel the Lamanite and Nephi claimed belief and then chose to walk more circumspectly before God?

Day 278, 3 Nephi 1:1-14

Consider not only verses 1-3, but all of the detailed accounts about the gold plates and their record keepers. These items are the best documented in the Book of Mormon. For me, this carefully produced record keeping is another proof of actual plates and not some fictitious fabrication.

With greater miracles and signs comes greater uproar and persecution (:4-9). In the midst of this great drama, the real question comes forth: Is faith worthless (:6, and 8)? Do you believe that the only way to validate faith is to prove, in a majestic showdown, that the beliefs of the unbeliever are vain? Or, can you see the value of your faith even when there are no external or quantifiable proofs of its benefits?

Which lessons are we supposed to learn from verses 10-14 about the following themes: prayer, trials, deliverance, prophets, cheerfulness, submission, and Atonement?

Day 279, 3 Nephi 1:15-30

In verses 15-22, you will see the fulfillment of all of the prophecies regarding the birth of Jesus Christ. Why do you think it is important to know that all of the prophecies about His birth were fulfilled, especially when we consider all of the prophecies regarding the last days and His promised second coming?

As you read verses 22-30, look for all the different kinds of problems and struggles that arrived after the astounding sign of the Savior's birth. What were some of the reasons why there were struggles when such a remarkable sign had been given?

What problems have you see arise when people "become for themselves" (:29)? What problems and struggles have happened when you have become for yourself? What will you "become for others" today, and how will that bless both them and you?

Day 280, 3 Nephi 2

As you read verses 1-3, ponder about whether a sign or a miracle does any good if it is not remembered. Are there any signs or miracles in your life that have lost some of their significance because of familiarity?

Sometimes people use the wording of verse 15 to promote and proclaim examples of racism in the Book of Mormon and LDS theology. Those who do are missing the larger context. This chapter deals with the unity of people who have different cultures and traditions, and also have different colored skin. These groups found unity as they battled the common enemy of wickedness and the rise of the Gadianton robbers (:11-18). Notice that the Lamanites called the Nephites their brothers in verse 12, and are even eventually called Nephites (:16). The language of verse 15 is not to be understood as doctrinally significant. It was the language and interpretation of a specific culture and time. To learn more about how the Book of Mormon is a fantastic example of unifying people of racial differences, read Ahmad Corbitt's article, "He Denieth None That Come unto Him: A Personal Essay on Race and the Priesthood, Part 3." You can find it on the Church's official church history website, history.lds.org. Seriously, take the time to look it up and read it. I promise that it will inspire you and help you see the Book of Mormon in a whole new light.

Day 281, 3 Nephi 3:1-10

What if Satan wrote you a letter trying to get you to surrender your beliefs and join his side? What might that be like? With a little name substitution and imagination, verses 1-10 can give us an idea of what that would be like. Enjoy and have a little fun with it.

People often tell the joke about a member of the Church who, just after giving a copy of the Book of Mormon to a friend, said, "You have to read 3 Nephi 3:7, it's the best!" accidentally saying 3 Nephi instead of 1 Nephi.

Why do you think Satan would want us to surrender rather than fight? What principles and ground is he trying to get our country, community, and families to surrender?

Day 282, 3 Nephi 3:11-26

Yesterday, Lachoneous received a letter from Giddianhi, the leader of the Gadianton Robbers. In verses 11-19, look for what Lachoneous does to prepare his people both spiritually and physically. Why do you think it is important to have both kinds of preparations?

In verse 19, the Nephites selected a great prophet to lead their armies. What advice did he give them in verses 20-21 regarding the demonstration of aggression and defense?

Day 283, 3 Nephi 4:1-14

How did the strategy of the Nephites in verses 1-6 strengthen them and weaken the robbers? Why do you think it is important not to give or leave the enemy of our soul anything that could be used against us? Why do you think it is important that we fight our battles based on the conditions that we have created?

In verses 7-10, look for what the robbers did to try to make the Nephites afraid of them. How well did their plan work? In what way is the adversary trying to make you afraid right now in your life? What have you learned from the Nephites about how to respond to these attempts?

Day 284, 3 Nephi 4:15-26

As you read verses 15-27, discover all of the different ways that the Nephites used the principles of preparation and gathering to help them in their war against the robbers. What are some ways that you have used the principles of preparation and gathering to protect and defend your family and yourself? What preparations do you think are going to be necessary in the future?

In verses 28-29, the Nephites give us a very interesting object lesson.

The gush of thankfulness and gratitude toward God by the Nephites in verses 30-33 is inspiring. For which blessings and events can you gush out your thankfulness to God today?

Day 285, 3 Nephi 5:1-19

Because of what the Nephites knew and did not doubt (:1-2), look for what they were willing to do in verse 3. What good things has your knowledge of the gospel, and not your doubts, caused you to do lately?

How do you think the Nephites were able to come up with such an interesting prison system for the captured robbers in verses 4-6?

For hundreds of pages and hundreds of abridged years, the prophet Mormon has been our silent guide. In verses 12-19, Mormon introduces himself, for the first time, to the readers of the book that bears his name. What significant but subtle lessons do these verses teach us about being disciples of Jesus Christ?

Day 286, 3 Nephi 5:20-6:18

The words "as the Lord liveth" are used for serious discussions (3 Nephi 5:24, and 26). These words mean that there is something so important that if it doesn't happen, then God would lose His Godhood. Look in 3 Nephi 5:20-26 for what is so important that if it doesn't happen, God ceases to exist.

After the defeat of the robbers, the Nephites begin to rebuild and prosper, as described in 3 Nephi 6:1-9. In fact, Mormon claimed that only wickedness and transgression could "hinder the people from prospering continually" (3 Nephi 6:5). This peace and prosperity was enjoyed for "but a few years" (3 Nephi 6:16). Look for all the different forms and ways that pride dominated their lives in 3 Nephi 6:10-18.

Out of all of the different ways that you saw pride manifested among the Nephites, which one also rears its nasty head in your life? In what ways has your pride robbed you of the peace you might have enjoyed?

Day 287, 3 Nephi 6:19-30

I love this line from verse 20: "And there began to be men inspired from heaven ..." Are you receiving enough inspiration from your prayers, study, worship, and pondering that you would consider yourself to be a woman or man who is inspired from heaven?

As you read verses 19-23, look for how these inspired people testified and how they were treated because of their testimonies.

What the priests, lawyers, and judges were doing was illegal. In verses 24-30, you will see how their covenants with each other allowed them to do these things. Temple covenants, in contrast, are for our benefit and the benefit of others. For those of you who have been through the temple, consider each of the temple covenants and how living it has blessed yourself and others.

Day 288, 3 Nephi 7:1-13

In today's section, we will see a complete collapse of the Nephite government and the rise of tribal culture.

In verse 10, we get this phrase regarding Jacob: "who had given his voice against the prophets who testified of Jesus." What will you give your voice for or against today?

Jacob also got many people to join his tribe and kingdom, "for he flattered them that there would be many dissenters" (:12). I can't help but think that Satan also made a similar claim. The number of believers or unbelievers should never outweigh a person's personal conviction and feelings. We will stay because we love the Lord and not because of multiplying membership.

Day 289, 3 Nephi 7:14-26

How well do the last few lines of verse 14 describe our day regarding: peace, hearts, and the treatment of prophets?

In verses 15-26, we get one of the most powerful and concise ministries of all time. Look for what you love about Nephi's qualifications, methods, miracles, and results.

What great thing will you do this week "in the name of Jesus" (:19, and 20)?

How does Nephi's example build your own confidence and capability to fulfill what you have been asked to do?

Day 290, 3 Nephi 8

This chapter contains an account of the destruction that accompanied the death of Jesus Christ.

In what ways do you think verses 20-23 are a good description of what the world would be like without a Savior?

Why do you think the Nephites were given such drastic signs and evidences of Christ's death when compared to what happened in Jerusalem (see Matthew 27:51, 54)?

Verses 24-25 contain a very regretful attitude about not repenting. We do not want to face a similar situation. To help us avoid this Elder Dallin H. Oaks has said, "What if the day of His coming were tomorrow? If we knew that we would meet the Lord tomorrow—through our premature death or through His unexpected coming—what would we do today? What confessions would we make? What practices would we discontinue? What accounts would we settle? What forgivenesses would we extend? What testimonies would we bear? If we would do those things then, why not now?" ("Preparation for the Second Coming," Ensign, May 2004, 9)

Day 291, 3 Nephi 9

In verses 1-12, we get an explanation from the Savior citing the reasons that He destroyed many of the cities and people of the Nephites and Lamanites. What do these reasons listed by the Savior teach us about what is really important to him? What value do we place upon these same things?

Notice how often the word "I" is used in these verses. The Lord makes no excuses. It was the people's wickedness that caused them to be destroyed, but He was the one who issued the justice. The Savior is kind and merciful to those who seek it, and demanding of those who don't.

After speaking about those who were destroyed, the Lord addresses His remarks to those who have survived. In verses 13-22, look for what the Savior's invitation is to those who survived. What must the people do to receive what He wants to give them?

Day 292, 3 Nephi 10

In verses 1-7, the Savior's voice is heard again. What significant thing does He teach the people about chickens? How are the words in verses 4-6 similar, and how are they different?

Verse 7 is a serious warning. What must we do, according to verses 6-7, to heed the Savior's warning?

When have you recently felt the change mentioned in verse 10 in your own life?

Mormon mentions that the people are about to have "great favors shown" and "great blessings poured out upon" them (:18). We will study these great blessings and favors in the coming days, and, if we are careful and prayerful, we will be able to see and feel the great blessings and favors that the Lord is going to pour out upon our own lives.

Day 293, 3 Nephi 11:1-17

In verses 1-7, Heavenly Father will help a group of people become increasingly aware and discerning of spiritual things. What lessons can we learn from theses verses about how to better recognize spiritual messages?

As Jesus Christ introduces himself to the people, what do you think are the most important ideas and concepts that He chooses to emphasize in verses 8-12? Why do you think each of those ideas and concepts are not only important to know, but also essential?

In verse 14, the Savior invited the whole multitude to come forth and feel His wounds so "that ye may know that I am the God of Israel, and the God over the whole earth, and have been slain for the sins of the world." In what way have verses 13-17 helped you come to realize the Lord's promise for yourself?

Day 294, 3 Nephi 11:18-41

In verses 18-28, look for what the Savior declares about baptism and who can perform this ordinance.

Truly, one of the hardest skills to develop is the ability to communicate with other people. How has verse 29 and the principle taught therein helped you in your relationships with others? Which relationship of yours will benefit today because of this verse?

In verses 28-41, look at how simply Christ explains His doctrine so there doesn't need to be any contention. After reading these verses, what would you say are the essential elements of His doctrine?

I love to draw out verse 32 on a piece of paper with the members of the Godhead in a triangle. Then, as I read the verse, I draw an arrow from one to another as they bear record of each other. In this very chapter, we are shown an example of this in verses 3-7 and 11.

Day 295, 3 Nephi 12:1-20

In verses 1-12, the Savior lists several attitudes and characteristics that will lead to increased happiness and blessings. Many of the blessings for obtaining these attitudes are mentioned in these verses, but in verses 1-2 Jesus mentions that the people would be blessed if they did additional things. What are the things He wants them to do? What blessings have you received for following the counsel in those verses?

In verses 13-16, both salt and a light are used to instruct followers of Christ about their responsibility to bless the world. When have you seen someone help or hurt others' belief in the gospel because of their actions? How do you feel about being asked to be light and salty?

In Christ's fulfillment of the law, many changes to policies and practices will take place, but the essential elements of what it means to come unto Him are unchanging. Look for some of these unchangeable elements in verses 17-20.

Day 296, 3 Nephi 12:21-48

What are some of the reasons that you believe Christ felt comfortable including himself in the wording of verse 48, considering He is absent from the Matthew 5:48 version?

In verses 21-47, Christ is not going to list everything we need to do. He is going to describe Christ-like characteristics that would cause us to think, feel, and act more like Himself and His Father in several situations. What characteristics can you see that they would like us to practice?

Which one of these teachings has helped you to think, feel, or act more like Heavenly Father and Christ?

Day 297, 3 Nephi 13

In the last chapter, we received a commandment to become perfect like Heavenly Father and Jesus Christ as well as instruction about the attitudes that would help us to act, feel, and think more like them. In today's chapter, we will be warned about hypocrisy and the danger it poses to our divine development. In verses 1-18, look for the rewards hypocrisy gives and takes away from us. If this is true with our donations, prayers, and fasting, what are some other gospel principles that could be affected by hypocrisy?

How could the teachings about treasures and service in verses 19-24 help or hinder us in the development of divine character?

Jesus's counsel in verses 25-34 is given to His ordained disciples, who are expected to dedicate their time, talents, and possessions in a full-time manner, similar to the way a General Authority would today. In what way have you also felt the fulfillment of these promises in your own life as you have sought to put "the kingdom of God and his righteousness" (:32) first?

Day 298, 3 Nephi 14

In addition to the danger of hypocrisy destroying our divine development, Jesus today adds a warning about misusing judgment. Verses 1-2 and their equivalent in Matthew 7:1-2 are among the most misunderstood of all of Jesus' teachings. Many believe that Jesus taught not to judge, but that is not what this whole chapter is trying to say. Instead of not judging at all, Jesus is trying to teach us how to judge righteously, which is exactly what He says.

As you read each of the following selections of verses, look for what Jesus is teaching us about how to judge better (:3-5, 6, 7-11, 12, 13-14, 15-20, 21-23, and 24-27).

Day 299, 3 Nephi 15

Some of the people that Jesus Christ appeared to and taught, believed that the Law of Moses was a vital and important part of their salvation. In verses 1-10, look for what Christ says about fulfilling the Law of Moses and about what He really wants from those who seek to keep the Law (:1, 9-10). Today, do all your normal faithful things, but make sure you do them with faith in Christ, and not just to check off a box.

A commentary by a scholar is good, a commentary by a prophet is better, but a commentary by Jesus Christ is the best. In verse 11-24, Jesus explains what John 10:11-16 means. How is this a good example of how the scriptures can be unlocked and unfolded to those who are humbly awaiting further light?

Day 300, 3 Nephi 16

Yesterday, the Nephites learned that Jesus spoke of them during His ministry in Israel (John 10:11-16). Today, the Nephites will learn that they are not the only ones to whom those verses apply. What does Jesus teach about these "other sheep" in 3 Nephi 16:1-3? What did Jesus say His purpose was in appearing unto them? Do you think the Second Coming can serve a similar purpose?

Verses 4-20 contain an remarkable prophecy about the House of Israel and the Gentiles. As you read these verses, try to determine where you think we are right now in this prophecy.

Day 301, 3 Nephi 17:1-20

According to verses 1-4, what roles do pondering and prayer have in coming to understand Jesus' teachings? How might these two principles help your learning experience next time you attend a church meeting?

Verses 4-20 are some of the most tender in all of scripture. Many of you have read these verses before. I invite you to ponder and pray your way through these verses today, looking, searching, and feeling for greater understanding about the Savior's compassion. What new understanding or feelings did you have?

What tender experiences have you and your family had with the Savior?

Prayer is meant to transform and change us. Look for how even Jesus ascended to a new level when He prayed in verses 15-18.

Day 302, 3 Nephi 17:21-18:14

In 3 Nephi 17:21-25, Jesus sends angels to surround and minister to the little children. I believe that the ministry of angels to surround and bless us is far more frequent than we think. If we are careful in our pondering, we may even be privileged enough to remember times revealed to us when mortal and heavenly angels were sent to surround and minister to us and our families.

In 3 Nephi 18:1-14, Jesus introduces the ordinance of the sacrament to the Nephites. Odds are that you have partaken of this ordinance many times. Here are a couple of words and phrases that I think would be worth your time to ponder as you study: "filled" (:4-5, 9), "one be ordained among you, and to him will I give power that he shall break bread and bless it unto the people of my church" (:5), "always" (:6, 11-12), "remembrance/remember" (:7, 11), "testimony/witness" (:7, 10-11), and "if" (:7, 12, 14).

Day 303, 3 Nephi 18:15-39

In verses 15-24, the Savior instructed His disciples and the members about how to pray and for whom to pray. How might you pray differently today because of this instruction?

Verses 25-34 contain instruction to those who were given authority to administer the sacrament and how to minister to those who are unworthy to partake. How hopeful is verse 32? As you read it, who was the person that you hoped would one day return?

Verses 36-39 are there to show us that the disciples also received authority to bestow the gift of the Holy Ghost. Ordinances are important and are expected to be performed by those with authority.

Day 304, 3 Nephi 19:1-14

In verses 1-3, look for all of the effort the people were willing to put forth to make sure others were able to come to Christ the next day. Who would you have made sure was invited? In what ways have you recently attempted to invite others to come to Christ?

In verse 4, we get the names of the 12 disciples that Jesus called and to whom He gave authority. How many sets of brothers were there? What name is shared by two of them? In verses 5-14, look for great principles of leadership that these disciples display.

I love the way the disciples prayed and what they prayed for in verse 9. When was the last time you prayed for what you "most desired" (:9)? Perhaps the reason there is not more heavenly fire/glory encircling us is that we are not praying for those things for which we should be praying (:14).

Day 305, 3 Nephi 19:15-36

In verses 15-23, Jesus again appears to the people and commands them to pray, but rather than praying to the Father they pray to Jesus. Look for what Jesus says about why the people were praying to Him. Is Jesus critical or understanding of their mistake?

I think that verse 24 is one of the most instructive in all of scripture about what it means to pray by the spirit. What difference do you feel when your personal prayers come from inspired thoughts and feelings rather than following a checklist? The next time you pray, will you try to pray for the things that Heavenly Father wants you to ask for and be grateful for?

As Jesus has seen and heard these incredible faith filled prayers, look for evidence of how this makes Him feel and what He is able to do for them because of their prayers in verses 25-36. Do you think Jesus "smiles upon" your personal and family prayers?

Day 306, 3 Nephi 20:1-22

The first of verse 1 may sound a little out of place when the Savior "commands the multitude that they should cease to pray," but it is the second part of the verse that I believe teaches us the key to having a great experience in any meeting. Applying this principle for ourselves and others will make sure that we are not just in a meeting with our brothers and sisters, but also in a meeting with Heavenly involvement. Check out this quote by Elder Bernard: "If I had the wish of my heart, I would remove from the vocabulary of the Latter-day Saints the word 'meeting'. We have not been talking about a 'Ward Council Meeting'. We have been talking about a 'revelatory experience' with the members of the Ward Council. If members of councils, if members of families as they come together, would think in terms of 'I'm preparing to participate in a revelatory experience with my family' instead of going to a meeting—a revelatory experience with a Ward Council—I think we would prepare and act much differently. In these latter days, given the forces of the adversary and darkness, no one person in a family and no one person in a ward are going to be the conduit through which all of the answers will come. So, all of that speaks to the spiritual nature of this work and seeking for the inspiration to do what the Lord wants us to do." (David A. Bednar. "Panel Discussion" Worldwide Leadership Training Meeting November 2010).

What do you think would have made the administering of the sacrament in verses 2-9 such an unbelievable experience?

The Savior invites the people to search the words of Isaiah for the prophecies that are to be fulfilled (:10-11). He then makes an marvelous prophecy in verses 12-22 about this people's remnant, the Gentiles, the land, the covenant, and New Jerusalem. Look for words like: "then," "if," and "I will."

Day 307, 3 Nephi 20:23-46

As you read verses 23-27, look for what they say about Jesus Christ. Look for specific lines that contain significant truths.

Christ fulfilled the covenant Heavenly Father made to provide a Savior and Atonement. The responsibility to share this incredible message was placed upon the early Jewish Christians and then the Gentiles. In verses 27-46, there is a prophecy about the scattering of Israel and the need to gather. Look for the word "then" and how it moves the prophecy, covenant, and timeline along.

What part do you think you will play in the fulfilling of this prophecy and covenant? Have you, like the Savior, covenanted to play a part in this prophecy?

Day 308, 3 Nephi 21

3 Nephi 20 established the need to gather scattered Israel. 3 Nephi 21 tells about how scattered Israel will be gathered. In verses 1-10 we learn that the Book of Mormon is both the sign and the tool for the gathering of Israel.

The phrase "these things" means the Book of Mormon in verses 2-4, and 7.

In verses 11-21, look for what will happen to those who reject the great and marvelous work of restoring the gospel and gathering Israel.

Yesterday, we were introduced to the first great separating question in 3 Nephi 20:23 "Do I believe Jesus is the Christ?" Today, we get the second great separating question in 3 Nephi 21:11 "Do I believe that Joseph Smith, the Book of Mormon, and the restoration are the work of God or man?"

In verses 22-29, look for what is promised to those who believe and receive the restored gospel.

Day 309, 3 Nephi 22

In the previous two chapters, Jesus spoke of the scattering and the gathering of His covenant people. In this chapter, He quotes from Isaiah 54. Look for how Isaiah compares the sorrow, loneliness, and heartbreak of being scattered, and then shows the incredible promises of redemption. The Lord's covenant people will be compared to a tent, a barren woman, and a forsaken wife. All of Israel's deficiencies will be made up through the kindness of their Lord. Read these verses slowly; read them out loud; and pray that you will feel the power of their truthfulness.

Look for what verses 1-3 say about the growth that Zion will experience someday.

In verse 11, what does the Lord, through Isaiah, promise will depart and be removed before His covenant and kindness?

There are forces in this world who seek to destroy faith in God, Jesus Christ, His prophets, and His Church. What do verses 15-17 say about such efforts?

Day 310, 3 Nephi 23

In verses 1-5, look for the reasons that Jesus "commanded" the people to "search" the words of Isaiah and the prophets.

Why do you think the commandment is to search the scriptures and words of prophets and not just read them?

What is the difference you have experienced by keeping the commandment to search the scriptures and the words of the prophets rather than just reading them?

What does the story in verses 6-13 teach you about the creation of scriptures and the involvement of both the human and the divine in this process?

What are some of the ways that Jesus continues to "expound" the scriptures unto you, and what does He expect/command us to do when He has expounded them(:6, and 14)?

Day 311, 3 Nephi 24-25

To help the Nephites to be ready for the time of judgment, Jesus quotes Malachi 3-4. As you read 3 Nephi 24, look for what it says about who will be able to abide the day of Christ's coming and who will not be able to abide it.

In 3 Nephi 24:8-12, we find that the law of tithing is one of the solutions to help us be worthy of abiding the judgment of the Second Coming. In what ways has God proven Himself to you through the significant and subtle blessings of tithing?

For those who believe that God's judgment and justice is lacking in this world, or that the righteous are rarely rewarded, check out the promises in 3 Nephi 24:13-18.

In 3 Nephi 25:1, we learn that the wicked will lose both the roots and branches of their family trees unless they apply 3 Nephi 25:5-6. What do the verses in D&C 128:17-18 add to your understanding?

Day 312, 3 Nephi 26

As you read verses 1-7, look for what Jesus expounded to the Nephite people.

It is interesting to go back to 3 Nephi 11 and count up chapters, pages, and verses and then multiply it by 100 to represent what we could have had (:6). What do verses 8-12 suggest about why we don't have more of this record, and what must happen before we can get more?

A summary of this majestic ministry of the Savior is found in verses 13-21. Every verse contains a great lesson or example. For which experience do you wish you could read the full account?

Day 313, 3 Nephi 27:1-12

After the ministry of Jesus Christ, the disciples united in mighty prayer and fasting to seek an answer to a question. Search verses 1-8 to identify the disciples' question and how the Savior answered it. What does this episode teach you about obtaining revelation to answer your questions?

Search verses 8-12, and then complete these phrases:
"The true Church of Jesus Christ must be . . ."
"Being a member of the Church of Jesus Christ is important to me because . . ."

Day 314, 3 Nephi 27:13-33

In verse 13, Jesus said He would give us His gospel. Then, in verse 21, He concluded that His gospel had now been taught. As you search verses 13-21, look for how you would describe the gospel of Jesus Christ. The culmination of living the gospel of Christ can be found in the expectation of verse 27.

What connection is made between writing and judgment in verses 22-27?

Look for what causes joy and sorrow for the Savior in verses 30-32.

Day 315, 3 Nephi 28:1-24

As you read verses 1-11, look for what each of the twelve disciples desired of the Savior. How did their desires determine what happened to them? What desires do you have that will determine your destiny?

There are many folk tales about the three Nephites. Search verses 7-10 and 16-23 for what we can learn about translated beings and their ministry.

Obviously, to a different degree than the three Nephites, you have been changed by your desires to preach the gospel to others. What are some of the transformations that have happened to you because of your desire to share the gospel?

Day 316, 3 Nephi 28:25-40

Why do you think Mormon wasn't allowed to write the names of the three Nephites (:25), when we know they come from those listed in 3 Nephi 19:4?

As you search verses 25-35, look for those to whom the three Nephites will minister, and what will be the impact of their teaching? Won't it be fun to one day be able to hear or read an accounting of their missionary report?

Verses 36-40 contains an answer to a question about the nature of the three Nephites that Mormon didn't know in verse 17. You can see what these verses teach you about translated beings. You can also ponder about what these verses teach you about receiving answers to doctrinal questions.

Day 317, 3 Nephi 29-30

In 3 Nephi 29, Mormon informs the reader that the Book of Mormon will one day come forth to the world. Look for the phrases "ye may know" and "ye need not" to help us understand what we are to know because of the Book of Mormon coming forth, and what we are not to do.

The word "wo" means deep sadness and regret. The word "spurn" means to disregard, reject with disdain or contempt. How do these definitions help unlock what this chapter is saying?

Chapter 30 is only two verses long. In verse 1, Mormon tells us he was commanded by Jesus Christ to write the words of verse 2. Look for the invitation and promise that Jesus Christ makes in verse 2 to those who have not made a covenant with Him. Have you taken the Lord up on His invitation, and have you received His promise?

Day 318, 4 Nephi 1:1-23

The 200-year period following the appearance and ministry of Jesus Christ among the Nephites is one of the happiest in the earth's history. Search verses 1-18 to discover the different elements that led to this fantastic time of peace and happiness.

Which of those elements have you regularly made a part of your life? Which of the elements mentioned have remained elusive and harder to obtain in your life and family? Will you practice one of these elements today and obtain some of that promised happiness?

What do you think would be the modern day equivalent to "ites" (:18)?

Why do you think the choices in verse 20 would lead to an eventual corruption of this incredible time of happiness?

Day 319, 4 Nephi 1:24-49

Yesterday, we saw principles of truth that, when lived, led to one of the happiest times in the history of the world. Search today's section for what caused this once great society to collapse.

Was there anything that you discovered that surprised you? What didn't surprise you?

Do you think Satan's strategy for destroying individuals, families, and societies has changed much?

Which verses do you think are good warnings for which you and your family should be aware?

Day 320, Mormon 1

As you read verses 1-5, look for the reasons why Ammoron trusted the young 10-year-old Mormon with the sacred records. For which sacred things has God entrusted you to be responsible? What does that tell you about His trust in you?

As war starts again between the Nephites and Lamanites, look for what stops in verses 8-14. What blessings have you lost recently because of fighting?

The age of 10 is a very unusual time to receive a calling. Look for what made Mormon's whole ministry unique in verses 15-19. Why do you think that was the instruction he got about preaching the gospel?

Day 321, Mormon 2:1-16

In verses 1-9, we have an account of Mormon's early command of the Nephite army. How well do you think he did? How do your early attempts at leadership compare with Mormon's?

As you search verses 10-15, look for the difference between sorrow, mourning, and lamenting versus real repentance. When have you experienced the difference between these two options? What would you say to someone to encourage them to add real repentance to his lamenting? When have you seen someone change her life through repentance?

Day 322, Mormon 2:17-29

Mormon gets the plates of Nephi, and begins to make an account of his own record. In verses 1-2, look for how the wickedness of others caused Mormon to feel. Is sin ever really an isolated experience? What about righteousness?

In verses 20-26, Mormon gathers, fortifies, urges, and arouses his army to fight with vigor as they defeat an army of 50,000 with only 30,000. Look for why this is not an occasion for great rejoicing in verses 26-27. Have you ever felt the difference between being successful while being left to yourself versus successful in the strength of the Lord?

Do you feel it diminishes our achievements to admit when the Lord has helped us accomplish something we couldn't do on our own? What tasks do you currently need strength from the Lord to accomplish?

Day 323, Mormon 3

In verses 1-8, the Nephites defeat the Lamanite armies twice. Then in verses 9-16, look for how the Nephites, Mormon, and the Lord feel about the victories. From these different feelings, what can we learn about how to be successful in our successes?

Mormon was an "idle witness" because the people would not accept his witness, and not because he wouldn't share it (:16). Which type of idle witness will you become?

According to verses 17-22, why and for whom does Mormon write? Did anything about Mormon's audience or scope of his writing surprise you?

Day 324, Mormon 4

Mormon 4 covers 13 years of multiple battles and the eventual loss of the Nephite land. In the midst of these blood-filled verses, there is a very sobering verse about wickedness and punishment. What is the message/warning in verse 5?

How do we surrender our power when we go on the offensive and seek to harm and hurt others (:4)?

In verses 14-15 and 21, the Lamanites, in celebration of their victories, offer the Nephite women and children as sacrifices to their idols. These are cringe-inducing accounts that would shock us today. Satan is not so bold as to seek for the blood of women and children to be dripping from altars today. Instead, he demands the sacrifice of women and children as he seeks their emotional, physical, and spiritual destruction. When you think of all the things in our world that cause such harm, it is obvious that this form of false worship is abundant. Sister Julie B. Beck has said, "Any doctrine or principle our youth hear from the world that is anti-family is also anti-Christ. It's that clear" ("Teaching the Doctrine of the Family," Ensign, March. 2011).

Is there any habit, belief, addiction, behavior, or speech that is causing the sacrifice of the women and children in your life?

Day 325, Mormon 5:1-12

In verses 1-2 look for who does and doesn't repent. Which of these repentances was necessary? Why do you think that a life without repentance would be a struggle?

Notice how careful Mormon is when writing in verses 8-9 about the violence and carnage he witnessed. What do you think Mormon might say about the violence that is available today for entertainment purposes?

There are great hints in verses 9-12 that one of Mormon's audiences is you. In what ways have you demonstrated "care for the house of Israel" (:10)? Do you "realize and know from whence ... [your] blessings come"(:10)? Do you "sorrow" for the "calamity" and "destruction" the Book of Mormon people (:11)?

In verse 12 ,we learn that the Lord commanded this record to be hid up because "wickedness will not bring them forth." What have you done, and what will you do, to bring forth the record of the Book of Mormon to others?

Day 326, Mormon 5:12-6:5

In Mormon 5:12-13, we learn that the Lord will bring forth the record of the Book of Mormon in his own time. In verses 14-15, look for what will be accomplished by bringing forth the Book of Mormon. Has the Book of Mormon fulfilled everything that it was prophesied it would?

After reading Mormon 5:15-20, complete each of the following phrases: "When the Spirit ceases to strive with people they . . ." "People who will not heed the Spirit are compared to things that have no control because . . ."

Answer Mormon's questions in Mormon 5:22-23, and then heed the warning in verse 24.

Day 327, Mormon 6:6-22

The sacred plates are transferred from Mormon to Moroni (:6). What have you done to transfer your beliefs and feelings about the sacred scriptures to your children?

How could the account in verses 7-8 have been different if their faith and faithfulness would have been stronger?

Verses 9-15 give an account of this last battle and the almost numberless carnage that came from it. It is difficult to imagine such numbers. Remember that every name you read in these verse is a general who represents 10,000 people.

Mormon's final lament for his people is found in verses 16-22. As you read these verses slowly and carefully, will you ponder what you must do so that similar things are never said of you?

Day 328, Mormon 7:1-8:11

What did Mormon tell the remnants of the Lamanite people in Mormon 7 about that which we should know, believe, and do? You may want to make a list of what you find under each category.

The last great battle between the Nephites and the Lamanites was in A.D. 385 (Mormon 6:5). Moroni begins his writing in A.D. 400 (Mormon 8:6). As you read Mormon 8:1-11, look for what has happened in the fifteen years since the battle at Cumorah.

What evidence is there that Moroni was incredibly faithful in these lonely times? It is a very difficult test and trial to remain faithful when there are no saints or friends with whom to gather. In these lonely times, the Three Nephites ministered to both Mormon and Moroni. Ultimately, it doesn't matter who ministers to the lonely—one of the Three Nephites or you—so long as someone does. At this point, are you in need of ministering, or are you able to minister others? Who is someone who ministered to you in a moment of loneliness?

Day 329, Mormon 8:12-25

What does Moroni say about the faults and mistakes that can be found in the Book of Mormon in verses 12 and 17? What do you think would happen if a person spent a majority of his time looking for the flaws instead of the truths? On what are you going to choose to focus?

Verses 18-22 describe how committed the Lord is to fulfilling the covenants and promises He has made. He will even bring forth judgment against those who seek to destroy His work by saying the promised covenants will not be fulfilled. Search verses 23-25 to discover how the prayers of many different saints prepared the way for Joseph Smith and us to prosper. What blessings will you ask for today on behalf of your posterity?

It took Joseph Smith several years to be ready to live what verses 14-16 teach about how to bring the Book of Mormon to light. The poverty of Joseph's family and the temptation to use his spiritual gifts for gain was the cause of several annual interviews with the angel Moroni (see Joseph Smith History 1:46, 53-56, and 59-60). To bring the Book of Mormon to light, is to place it on display for others to come and examine its claims and truths for themselves. In what ways have you helped bring the Book of Mormon to light?

Day 330, Mormon 8:26-41

Yesterday, we learned that the Book of Mormon will come forth to fulfill the promises made to those faithful saints who prayed for its arrival. Today as you study, look for what Moroni says about the time and culture in which the Book of Mormon would come forth. Notice the phrase "come in a day" in several verses.

Check out verse 35 to see how Moroni was able to so accurately describe our time and day.

Once you have identified all of the problems that Moroni points out in our day, it is helpful to know that the Book of Mormon was brought forth in this time because it is the solution to each of these issues. Pick nearly any problem that exists in our world and then consider how a heartfelt study of the Book of Mormon will reveal the solutions to that problem. The same is also true about our lives. To which personal problems have you found solutions while studying the Book of Mormon?

Days 331, Mormon 9:1-21

In verses 1-6, Moroni speaks to those who don't believe in Christ. He doesn't try to convince them; instead he explains how one day they will not be able to doubt and why they would not be comfortable living in God's presence. What do verses 3-4 and D&C 88:29-36 help us understand about why God chooses to have degrees of glory rather than heaven or hell?

Verses 11-14 contain a great mini overview of the Plan of Salvation. What is taught about creation, the Fall, redemption, resurrection, and judgment in those verses?

We live in a world where miracles and the God who performs them are doubted. What does Moroni say in verses 7-10 and 15-21 to explain why miracles cease, and also why we can still expect them to happen? What miracles have you witnessed to convince you that God still performs miracles?

147

Day 332, Mormon 9:22-37

What did Jesus tell, not only to the Three Nephites, but to all disciples who seek to follow Him in verses 22-25? When have you felt that any of these promises have been "confirmed" to you (:25)?

"Despise" is an interesting word to describe the feelings of some toward their God in verses 26-27. Instead of maintaining their scornful dislike for God and His followers, what invitations do verses 27-29 make to these "despisers?" Do you think there is any value of an ordinance when one participates "unworthily" (:29)?

As you read verses 30-37, consider how aware Moroni is of his "imperfections," shortcomings, and mistakes. The Book of Mormon and the people whose lives it highlights are open about their imperfections, and yet they have been a force for accomplishing much good. Perhaps there is a lesson for us in the midst of this confession of imperfection? If the Lord can work a great restoration and conversion through an imperfect book and prophets, then what miracles and good works can he bring about today through you and me?

Day 333, Ether 1

The Title Page of the Book of Mormon says the book of Ether "is a record of the people of Jared, who were scattered at the time the Lord confounded the language of the people, when they were building a tower to get to heaven." What additional information do we get about this book in verses 1-5?

Verses 6-32 is one of those great genealogy lists that we love to read. Which of these names do you hope will be given to one of your grandchildren?

The word "confounded" means to be bewildered, confused, perplexed, even damned. As you study verses 33-43, look for how many times you can see the following principle being used: When we are confounded, we should cry unto the Lord in prayer, and He will have compassion upon us, our families, and our friends. When have you used this principle in your life? What is confounding you at this point in your life that should cause you to cry unto the Lord through prayer?

If you want your children to be raised up unto the Lord, then cry unto the Lord for a long time (:34).

Day 334, Ether 2:1-12

As you read verses 1-7, look for all of the effort that Jared, his brother, and their families made to travel where the Lord wanted them to go. Also, notice how much direction the Lord gave to this traveling group. Though the direction came, often it came through a cloud. Sometimes the communication from the Lord is cloudy and not as clear as we would like, but if we continue moving and following directions from the Lord, we will arrive in the Promised Land. How much do these verses show you that the Lord wants us to live with Him?

Verses 8-12 contain a prophetic promise regarding the blessing and cursing of the chosen land that the Jaredites, Nephites, Lamanites, and later the Gentiles will inhabit. What do these verses say about what must happen before the wrath of the Lord is poured out upon the people? Why do you think the Lord chooses to bless us for every little effort that we make, and curse us only when we reach a fullness?

Day 335, Ether 2:13-25

My wife, children, and I love going to the beach. Apparently, Jared and his brother did also. For four years they lived by the seashore (:13). In verses 14-15, look for what the brother of Jared had forgotten to do during that time and how the Lord felt about it. How well are you doing at the thing that the brother of Jared forgot to do? How long might be your conversation with the Lord about this topic?

The Lord never intended for Jared, his brother, and their families to remain on the beach in vacation mode. He wanted to lead them to a Promised Land, just as He wants to lead us to the Celestial kingdom. As you read verses 16-17, look for what the Lord instructed the brother of Jared to do to complete the next stage of their journey to the Promised Land? What instruction and work would the Lord have you and your family do to complete the next stage of your journey to His kingdom?

Verse 17 has a phrase that is used several times to describe the construction of these vessels. This type of construction, while good for keeping water out, has caused a couple of problems according to verses 18-19. The brother of Jared takes these problems to the Lord for help. Look for what

149

problems the Lord does and does not solve in verses 20-25. Why do you think the Lord didn't solve all of the problems?

Three times in verse 25, the Lord tells the brother of Jared and us that we have been prepared to successfully make the journey to the Promised Land. What evidence do you have that the Lord prepared you in your past for things that you would do and face?

Day 336, Ether 3:1-16

The problems of no air and steering were taken care of by the Lord, who then left the problem of no light to the brother of Jared. In verses 1-5, you will see the proposed solution for the "no light" problem. In these same verses, look for what the brother of Jared believes about his own abilities and how he feels about the ability of the Lord.

Elder Jeffrey R. Holland once told a group of mission presidents and their wives that if all we had from the Book of Mormon was the revelation that the brother of Jared received of Jesus Christ, it would be worth every effort to take it to the world. Meticulously read verses 6-16 and look for every incredible truth that is taught about Jesus Christ.

Verse 15 is intriguing and sometimes a little confusing. There are many theories and thoughts about what the wording may mean, but the one I like best comes from Elder Holland's book, *Christ and the New Covenant*. He interprets Christ as saying, "Never have I shown myself unto man in this manner, without my volition, driven solely by the faith of the beholder. As a rule prophets are invited into the presence of the Lord, are bidden to enter his presence by him and only with his sanction. The brother of Jared, on the other hand, seems to have thrust himself through the veil, not as an unwelcome guest but perhaps technically as an uninvited one... Obviously the Lord himself was linking unprecedented faith with this unprecedented vision. If the vision itself was not unique, then it had to be the faith and how the vision was obtained that was so unparalleled. The only way that faith could be so remarkable was its ability to take the prophet, uninvited, where others had been able to go only with God's bidding" (p.23). What do you love about this idea about how faith can pierce the veil?

Day 337, Ether 3:17-28

This year, we have seen two occasions where the Lord ministered unto two different groups of people (:17-18). What would your record of the Lord's personal ministries to you include?

Look for how the Lord instructs these sacred things to be treated and kept in verses 22-24 and 27-28. How well do you record and maintain the record of your sacred experiences?

Look for everything that the brother of Jared saw and came to know in verses 17-20 and 25-26. How can a person come to know something without seeing it?

Left to his own wit to solve the problem of no light, the brother of Jared brought rocks to the Lord. So unconfident was the brother of Jared in his hewed creation that he referred to them as "these things" when addressing the Lord (3:3). I love how the Lord takes these stones, representing the brother of Jared's efforts to solve a problem, and not only touches them so they shine, but declares that two of them will become one of the tools for translating the Book of Mormon and reserves them for the future purpose of translating the rest of the sealed portion of the plates (:21-24, 27-28). How many times have you taken an unconfident solution to a problem to the Lord, only to have Him touch it and turn it into a shining Urim and Thummim? What is the next problem that you need to humbly take to the Lord so that He can transform it into a tool to accomplish His work?

Sometimes people get upset that Joseph Smith used a seer stone in addition to the Urim and Thummim to translate the Book of Mormon. Without the Lord's help and touch, they are all just rocks. The Lord works with the "things" that we bring to Him. Don't be upset with the Lord for working with our stupidity, weakness, and foolishness, just be grateful that He does.

Day 338, Ether 4

What instruction did the brother of Jared, and later Moroni, receive regarding the sealed portion of the plates in verses 1-7? Are you helping us to get closer to receiving this record, or further away?

Verses 8-12 contain words directed toward those who believe and those who do not believe. According to verse 11, how will those who believe come to know that this record is true?

151

What invitations and promises does the Lord make to the Gentiles and House of Israel in verses 13-14?

We were told in verse 7 that we needed faith like the brother of Jared in order to receive the sealed portion of the plates. In verse 15, we learn how to "rend that veil of unbelief" by praying like the brother of Jared did, a lesson that is also taught in ancient and modern temples. Will you tear at the veil of unbelief today by offering the kind of prayer that we have just learned about?

In verses 16-19, we learn that the Book of Mormon is a sign that the revelation given to John the Beloved will be unfolded, and thus it should be a time of great repenting, covenant making, and covenant keeping so we may be blessed and lifted up.

Day 339, Ether 5:1-6:11

It appears that Moroni is giving direct counsel to Joseph Smith in verses 1-3. In addition to this counsel, look for how many different people Moroni says will witness that the Book of Mormon is true. You may want to make a list. How have the above witnesses helped you? Who else would you add to this list whose testimony of the Book of Mormon has helped you? Do you feel comfortable adding your name to the list you have made?

In chapter 6 verses 1-5, we see that everything has been prepared for the journey, and then comes this line: "commending themselves unto the Lord their God" (6:5). This pattern is the same for our lives, days, and hours. We do what we can to prepare and then commend ourselves to the Lord.

In verses 6-11 of chapter 6, the vessels are directed toward the Promised Land by an almost violent wind, which created monstrous waves. This wind comes from the Lord, according to verse 6. Why didn't the Lord blow softer? Why doesn't He protect us more from the painful and rough elements of life? He is driving us to the Promised Land. We need to know that only He can bring us forth from the inescapable depths if we call upon Him and sing praises of thanks when we are delivered (6:6-10).

Day 340, Ether 6:12-7:6

After arriving in the Promised Land, we get very little information about the life of the Jared and his brother. The family grows, and before these patriarchs die, their family wants them to appoint a king, which they do against the warning of the brother of Jared (6:20-30). The unheeded warning manifests itself in the very next chapter in verses 1-6.

In Ether 6:12, 17, and 30, look for what is taught about the importance of humility. Humility is essential in all learning; why is this an even more important quality if we want to be "taught from on high" (Ether 6:17)? This question may help us to more humbly notice the tender mercies from God: In what ways has my life been blessed by Thee that I haven't noticed, but for which it would be good for me to be grateful? Questions like that will often result in us being taught from on high.

Day 341, Ether 7:7-27

If you thought that your family had problems, then I would like to introduce you to the Jaredite families of Kib and Corihor. Enjoy keeping up with all of the names and problems that will present themselves in this chapter. The drama and action reads like a soap opera.

As you read, consider finding the things that made Shule a successful leader so that his people could prosper. Which of these discovered traits do you think will help you to avoid the drama and contention that was demonstrated so clearly by these families?

Day 342, Ether 8:1-18

Our Father in Heaven offers us all that He has if we will surrender our will to Him, keep the commandments of Jesus Christ, and follow the direction of the Holy Ghost (D&C 84:33-39). This kingdom and power is available to all, but most will not exercise the patience or enact the change that is necessary to obtain what is promised. In today's section, Jared is a great example of this. Look for how Jared and those associated with him seek to obtain fleeting power and kingdoms at the loss of the eternal and infinite.

What tactics did Jared and his daughter use to obtain what they wanted, and which of those are still highly effective now?

Day 343, Ether 8:19-26

In the last section, we saw how Jared and his daughter used secret combinations and oaths to create murderous plans and covenants. Read verses 19-26 to learn more about such practices and then answer the following questions:

153

How does God feel about secret combinations?

What are the goals of secret combinations?

What effect do secret combinations have on nations and societies?

What warning are we given regarding them?

What evidence can you find that such combinations exist in our day and in our culture?

Day 344, Ether 9:1-22

Secret combinations can be frightening, but look for how the Lord protected and preserved Omer and his family in verses 1-3. When has your family been protected and preserved by a revelation of warning?

Yesterday, we learned about the effects that secret combinations had and will have upon nations and society. In verses 4-12, look for the effects that secret combinations have upon the family of Jared. Verse 11 highlights the two major goals of secret combinations.

In verses 13-22, look for all of the blessings that came to the people under the direction of the righteous fatherhood and leadership of Omer and Emer.

The animals named in verse 19 have sometimes caused confusion and alarm; how can elephants be in the Americas, and what the heck are cureloms and cumoms? The dates on the extinction of mammoths and mastodons keeps getting nearer to that of the Jaredites, and in some cases, they are even dated as contemporaries. As for the cureloms and cumoms, these animals fall into the untranslated category. We don't know what exactly they are because they weren't described. Though there have been many wonderful thoughts and theories, in the end, we know very little from the text, so be patient with this unfolding question.

Day 345, Ether 9:23-35

After having a couple of righteous kings, Heth "began to embrace the secret plans...to destroy his father" (:26). In this verse, you can see the difference between the covenants of Satan and those of Heavenly Father and what this difference does to family relationships. In what ways is Satan tempting you to destroy your family? Heth embraced these plans. There is a difference between embracing and being tempted. What good and bad things have you embraced this week? What will you continue to embrace and what will you abandon?

It takes humility to recognize, repent, and then abandon those things which we should not have embraced during the week. Sufficient humbling of ourselves will always result in the raining of blessings from heaven (:35). How do you know when you are sufficiently humble?

In verses 28-34, look for some of the penalties enacted on the Jaredites because they refused to repent when the prophets asked. Are there any unnecessary struggles/serpents in your life because of unheeded prophetic counsel and warnings? If there are, then I invite you to have a sufficiently humbling experience when you partake of the sacrament this week.

Day 346, Ether 10:1-14

Look in verses 1-4 for the different things that Shez "built up." Do you think that the order of these things is significant? Who and what will you build up today?

Shez built, while Riplakish burdened his people with various things in verses 5-8. In what ways did Riplakish twist several ideas that could have been good into destructive forces?

Verses 9-12 contain the account of Morianton's leadership. In many ways, he built like Shez, but he was lacking in some aspects according to verse 11. How might the growth described in verse 12 be lacking the depth of the growth mentioned in verses 1-4?

In verse 13, Kim, the king next in line, "was not favored of the Lord." How do you know when you are in the Lord's favor?

Day 347, Ether 10:15-34

Verses 15-29 give an account of four different kings who did that which was right in the sight of the Lord and a detailed listing of their prosperity. In verse 28 the words "blessed," "prospered," and "choice" are used to describe the people and their land. What words would you use to speak about your own life and circumstances? What words do you think an ancient prophet would use to speak of your life and situation?

Without warning or explanation, the next six generations of kings and their people spend their lives in "captivity" (:30-31). What are some of the different ways that people find themselves in captivity today?

In order for Com to escape captivity, look for how long and hard he has to fight in verse 32, only to face a new threat in the form secret oaths in verse 33. Why do you think, even with much fighting, Com could not prevail against these oaths (:34)?

Day 348, Ether 11

This chapter will cover several years and leaders. Verses 1, 12, and 20 mention that there came "many prophets and prophesied" that destruction would come "except they should repent." How is the sending of many prophets, who call us to repentance, a witness that God deeply loves us? Who are a few of the many prophets that the Lord has sent to help you repent of something?

If a prophet of God were to sit down to counsel you, for what would they tell you to repent?

As you read this chapter, look for how the blessings or curses upon a land are tied to how receptive people are of prophets and their message. Who do you think more people are listening to today, the many prophets, or the mighty messengers of the secret combinations (:15-22)?

This week, how have you tried to obey the words of the prophets and claim some of their promised blessings?

Day 349, Ether 12:1-21

The amazing ministry of the prophet Ether begins in verses 1-3. What line indicates that he has a tenacious spirit?

In verse 4, Ether describes the effects of hope. This hope is not the worldly, wishy hope, but a deep surety born of belief that things will happen. Of the effects mentioned in verse 4, which could you testify that you have experienced?

In verse 6, Moroni begins to introduce the subject of faith. Then, in verses 7-21, Moroni shares several examples of faith throughout the scriptures. Which of these is your favorite story? What have you been able to accomplish through faith to add to this legacy of faith?

At the end of verse 6, Moroni said people will receive "no witness until after trial of" their faith. For each story of faith that was mentioned in verses 7-21, there was also a trial that had to be overcome. What trial are you going through or have gone through that will be useful in building your faith?

Day 350, Ether 12:22-41

In verses 22-25, Moroni again expresses his concern about his writing ability. What are the reasons that he is concerned? What does the Lord say and promise to do in verses 26-29 to alleviate Moroni's concern?

In what ways have you experienced the promise of verse 27 with your own weaknesses? What current weakness might you need to humbly take to the Lord?

In verse 28, Moroni said he would show how faith, hope, and charity can bring about all righteousness. Search verses 29-37 for what righteous things faith, hope, and charity caused in the past and can produce in the future.

What finial points does Moroni seek to make to the Gentiles as he bids them farewell in verses 38-41?

Day 351, Ether 13:1-18

Latter-day Saints believe "that Zion (the New Jerusalem) will be built upon the American continent" (Article of Faith 10). Look for what Moroni summarizes about Ether's teachings on the New Jerusalem and the Jerusalem of old in verses 1-12. Look for the major qualification of both cities in verses 10-11. What can Revelations 21:10-27, D&C 45:64-71, and Moses 7:61-65 add to our understanding of the New Jerusalem?

From the cavity of his hiding rock, Ether is able to document the destruction of the Jaredites. What are a few of the things that led to their destruction, according to verses 13-18? What will you do to make sure that those same things don't destroy you and your family?

Day 352, Ether 13:19-14:7

So much of what we will read about today is summed up in Ether 13:19. Some of the most frequent words in today's section are "battle," "fought," "anger," and "fight." What happens to relationships and homes if these are the frequent ideas and feelings in our own life? What words would you like to be frequently associated with your home and family?

The curse brought on by unrighteousness and unrepentant attitudes has caused the men to sleep with their swords in their "right hand" to defend their property, lives, and families (Ether 14:1-2). The right hand is a symbol of covenant making and keeping. Is a sword, gun, or attitude of fighting really the best way to defend and protect our families? What better things might we put into our right hand to protect our families?

Day 353, Ether 14:8-31

Look for what a person can expect from a life that is focused on gaining only power and possession.

Verse 18 is often laughed at by the youth of the Church. In verses 17, and 19-24, discover the reason for this fear that has overtaken the people. What feelings of gratitude do you have for living in a country that is free from such violence? What feelings of sorrow do you have for those places in the world where the fear of a modern day Shiz is real? Is there anyone in your life that fears you the way that these ancient people feared Shiz? If there is, how will you correct this?

Day 354, Ether 15:1-17

What results did Coriantumr receive for ignoring the prophets in verses 1-3? What evidence have you seen that no lasting happiness comes from ignoring prophets?

Look for the reasons that the people gathered together in verses 12-15. Those reasons are quite different from the reasons that people gather together in D&C 115:6. When have you experienced the blessings and promises of gathering together with the saints?

For four years, the people of Coriantumr and Shiz gathered together so that every night they could have what is described in verses 16-17. What feelings and experiences can you promise to those whom you invite to gather with you in worship?

Day 355, Ether 15:18-34

Verse 19 describes the feelings, desires, and changes that happened to the people because they lost the Spirit of the Lord. As you read verses 20-32, notice all the phrases that demonstrate the blindness and hardness of heart mentioned in verse 19.

Did you notice the lack of care and compassion for others the last time that you lost the Spirit of the Lord? When we lose the Spirit, we battle, we fight, and we sleep upon our swords, ready to awake to a battle and destroy the lives of those with whom we live, work, and associate.

Did you know that losing the Spirit of the Lord, puts your marriage, family, ward, town, and nation at risk? Will you strive a little harder to keep the Spirit of the Lord? Will you repent a little faster when you do something that causes the Spirit to leave? I will too, and all of our relationships will be blessed for it.

As a little boy, I remember reading and loving verses 29-32. I don't know what little girls think of those verses, but little boys love them, and most the older ones do too. Coriantumr and Shiz fought so hard to live and to take life. Now, compare that to the final words of the prophet Ether in verse 34. For what was he was fighting, hoping, praying, and living?

Day 356, Moroni 1-3

The great last battle between the Nephites and the Lamanites was in A.D. 385 (Mormon 6:4-5). The Book of Mormon ends in A.D. 421 (Moroni 10:1). That means that Moroni had several years when he was utterly alone. As you read Moroni 1:1-4, consider what his life must have been like. What lessons can we learn from Moroni about endurance, faithfulness, courage, and hope? It might have been much easier for Moroni to die for the gospel than to live it. There are two ways to give your life for Christ, and Moroni is a great example of how to do one while being willing to do the other.

Moroni is the last believer in Christ in his day, and yet he writes in the next few chapters what he hopes will "be of worth unto my brethren" (1:4). This lone man without a church and fellowship provides instruction on how to build and run a church after people are given authority. What does he say in chapters 2-3?

Day 357, Moroni 4-5

If a person is active and in good health, he or she would hear the sacrament prayers around 40-45 times a year. How many times do you think you have heard these prayers? Without looking, do your best to write down what you can remember of each prayer on a separate piece of paper. If you would like to memorize these prayers, you can write down one small phrase at a time, then repeat it out loud, and then continue adding one new phrase at a time, repeating after each new phrase.

Something that really helped me have a more intimate experience with the sacrament prayers, was replacing the pronouns "we," "they," and "those" with the personal pronouns I, and my. What difference does this exercise make in the way that you understand the personal nature of these prayers?

The word "witness" means to testify. How can partaking of the sacrament be a personal testimony meeting between you and the members of the Godhead?

What are the promises that both we and the Lord make in these ordinances? What are the differences between the prayers?

Why do you think we eat and drink to help us remember Christ rather than just looking at an image of Him or reading an account of Him?

Day 358, Moroni 6

On a scale of one to ten, where would you place your average church experience? Is your experience different depending upon which meeting you are in? As you read this chapter, look for things that will make church meetings more uplifting and powerful.

People sometimes make the argument that they are spiritual rather than religious. What does this chapter teach about the benefits of belonging to the Lord's Church?

What does verse 4 teach us about how to know when the Atonement is actively cleansing and forgiving our sins?

In verses 5-8, there are several things that we are told would happen "oft" among the saints. Why should these things be done with a frequent rapidity? What advantages and blessings have come into your life from frequent participation in these events?

Day 359, Moroni 7:1-19

Chapter 7 does not come from Moroni. Look in verses 1-5 to discover who is speaking and to whom he is speaking. Who would be the modern day audience for this talk?

Those people mentioned in verses 1-5 do much good. What do verses 6-11 reveal about the importance of doing the right thing for righteous reasons? What difference happens when we do good things with the right intent?

Verse 19 teaches that if we learn the difference between good and evil, and lay hold upon the good, then we will each become a child of Christ—meaning that we will become like Christ. It is essential to be able to discern good from evil in order to develop godliness. What are the key words, phrases, and ideas presented in verses 12-19 to help us do that? In our busy world, the choice is sometimes between good and evil, but much more frequently they are choices among good, better, and best. How can the principles from verses 12-19 help us with those choices?

Day 360, Moroni 7:20-34

To become like God and Christ we must "lay hold upon every good thing" (:19). What do verses 20-34 teach us about how to accomplish this?

What good things has your faith in Christ allowed you to lay hold of?

What good things will you use your faith in Christ to lay hold on in the coming year?

God has sent us scriptures, prophets, and miracles to help build our faith in Christ, so that we might lay hold of good things. Verses 29-34 focus on how the Lord has also used angels to do this.

Day 361, Moroni 7:35-48

In yesterday's section, we learned that God sent prophets, scriptures, angels, and miracles to help us lay hold upon good things. Verses 35-39 identify faith as the reason why God sends these helpers and the lack of faith as why He does not. Faith isn't simply belief; faith is doing something because of your belief. Was this last week short on miracles or faith?

Faith in Christ allows us to lay hold upon good things and leads us to have hope. Hope is not a weak wish, but a powerful motivating assurance that other good things will come (:40-44). This gift of God allows us to lay hold upon good things that will yet come, and to be strengthened, comforted, and assured right now. What are some of the things that you hope for on bad days?

Faith is manifest in action. Hope is found in assurances. Charity is a gift from God that directs how we do all things. The trio of faith, hope, and charity is doing the right things for the right reasons, in the right way. As you read verses 45-47, consider how everything you do would improve if done this way.

We know that charity is more than good feelings; it is the very character of Christ (:47). When in the last year has Christ manifested to you each of the attitudes listed in verses 45-47? Which of these attitudes will you need to demonstrate today? According to verse 48, what will help in that process?

Faith, hope, and charity, like every other gift of God, were sent to help us lay hold upon every good thing. As you look forward in faith to the completion of today, what assurances of hope are coming to your mind and heart because you will act in a charitable, Christlike way? That sounds like a pretty good day. Now, pray your guts out for it (:48).

Day 362, Moroni 8:1-26

This chapter is a letter from Mormon to Moroni after a recent appointment solving a doctrinal dispute. As you read verses 1-21, look for what the dispute was about and how Mormon addressed the dispute by teaching several important doctrines that were being misunderstood. What did Mormon teach about God, the Plan of Salvation, and the Atonement in his response?

Children are exempt from the demands of justice through the mercy of the Atonement. According to verses 22-24, who else is covered by the power of the Atonement?

Look for the pattern that those who are accountable because of age and knowledge are supposed to follow in verses 25-26.

Day 363, Moroni 8:27-9:19

In today's section, Mormon finishes one letter and starts another to Moroni outlining the depravity of the people. As you read, look for phrases that prove how degenerate the people had become. Which lines did you find to be the most horrific? If you did the exact opposite of those lines, rather than destroying the civility of a people, you would build it. In what ways has the nastiest of these people motivated you to do better?

Notwithstanding the hardness of others, what does Mormon teach us about what we are to do in verse 6?

How does tremendous evil actually build our faith and expectation in God's judgment (9:14-15)?

Day 364, Moroni 9:20-10:7

Mormon's last words are found in chapter 9 verses 20-26. What feelings and thoughts do these verses give you as he addresses his son?

In verse 21-22, Mormon mentions whom he can and cannot recommend to God. What parts of your life can be recommended to God by your loved ones? Is there any part of your life that cannot be recommended to God at this time?

In chapter 10 verses 1-7, we are given Moroni's promise concerning how to discover the truth of the Book of Mormon. As you carefully read these verses, look for the essential elements of the pattern. How would you list them? Why do you think each part is important?

What experiences have you already had using this pattern with the Book of Mormon? When have you used this pattern with other things? No matter how many times you may have already used this pattern, will you follow it again today, to inquire of the truthfulness of the Book of Mormon?

Day 365, Moroni 10:8-34

Rather than just looking at the spiritual gifts listed in verses 9-16, search verses 8 and 17-18 for why these gifts are given, and how they can be cultivated. What gifts have you been given to bless the lives of others? What is the next spiritual gift that God wants you to cultivate?

Among all of the spiritual gifts mentioned in this chapter, faith, hope, and charity are essential. What do verses 20-23 explain about why these gifts are necessary?
What do verses 19 and 24-30 say about why there is an absence of spiritual gifts? Why do you think there are more or fewer spiritual gifts in the world today?

As you have read about the wonderful gifts that are available, you have probably been prompted to improve. In verses 30-34, Moroni leaves us with his final instruction on how to use the Atonement of Jesus Christ to "lay hold upon every good gift," and thus achieve godliness (:30). These last four verses contain a lifetime of counsel on improvement efforts through Christ. At this point in your life, what gifts, skills, thoughts, and feelings does Christ want you to bring to Him for perfecting? What are the things that He wants you to deny yourself so that He can perfect what you bring?

Day 366

Because the gospel is endless, I invite you to continue in your efforts to study daily. You may want to consider another book in the Study Daily series. Thank you for allowing me to be a part of your sacred time each day.

Bibliography

Ballard. M Russell. "Let Us Think Straight." BYU *Campus Education Week*, Aug 20 2013.

Beck. Julie B. "Teaching the Doctrine of the Family." *Ensign*, March 2011.

Bednar. David A. "Honorably Hold a Name and Standing." *Ensign*, May 2009.

Bednar. David A. "Panel Discussion." *Worldwide Leadership Training Meeting*, Nov 2010.

Bednar. David A. "Quick to Observe." BYU *Devotional*, May 10 2005.

Bednar. David A. "Reaching Many 'Ones' in England." Retrieved from: https://www.lds.org/study/prophets-speak-today/unto-all-the-world/many-ones-taught-by-apostle-visiting-england?lang=eng&cid=email-shared

Bednar. David A. "The Tender Mercies of The Lord." *Ensign*, May 2005.

Bednar. David A. "To Sweep the Earth as with a Flood." *Campus Education Week at Brigham Young University*, Aug 2014.

Benson. Ezra Taft. *Teachings of the Presidents of the Church: Ezra Taft Benson.* Salt Lake City, Utah: The Church of Jesus Christ of Latter-day Saints, 2014.

Cook. Carl B. "It is better to look up." *Ensign*, Nov 2011.

Eyring. Henry B. "And Thus We See: Helping A Student In A Moment of Doubt." Address to CES Religious Educators, February 5 1993.

Eyring. Henry B. "In the Strength of the Lord." *Ensign*, May 2004.

Eyring. Henry B. "Prophecy and Personal Revelation." *Ensign*, April 2016.

Eyring. Henry B. "The Book of Mormon Will Change Your Life." CES symposium on the Book of Mormon, Aug 17 1990.

Godfrey. Kenneth W. "A New Prophet and a New Scripture: The Coming Forth of the Book of Mormon." *Ensign*. Jan 1988.

Hinckley. Gordon B. "Our Quest for Excellence" *Ensign*, Sep 2010.

Holland. Jeffrey R. *Christ and the New Covenant*. Salt Lake City, Utah: Deseret Book, 1997.

McKay. David O. "Dedicatory Prayer Delivered by President. McKay at New Zealand Temple." *Church News*, May 10 1958.

McConkie. Joseph Fielding, Millet. Robert L. *Doctrinal Commentary on the Book of Mormon, vol. 3*. Salt Lake City, Utah: Deseret Book, 1991.

Otterson. Michael R. "On The Record." *2015 FairMormon Conference*.

Packer. Boyd K. "Counsel to Youth." *Ensign*, Oct 2011.

Scott. Richard G. "Removing Barriers to Happiness." Ensign, May 1988.

Smith. Joseph F. *Gospel Doctrine*. Salt Lake City, Utah: Deseret Book, 1989.

Smith. Joseph. Jr. *Teachings of the Prophet Joseph Smith*. Salt Lake City, Utah: Deseret Book, 1976.

Uchtdorf. Dieter F. An address given in Kyiv, Ukraine conference, June 6 2009.

Uchtdorf. Dieter F. "Pride and Priesthood." *Ensign*, Nov 2010.

Made in the USA
San Bernardino, CA
23 July 2018